Also by John Updike

GOLF DREAMS

John Updike

GOLF DREAMS

WRITINGS ON GOLF

DRAWINGS BY PAUL SZEP

New York: Alfred A. Knopf

1996

THIS IS A BORZOI BOOK
PUBLISHED BY ALFRED A. KNOPF, INC.

Grateful acknowledgment is made to John Murray (Publishers) Ltd. for permission to reprint an excerpt from "Seaside Golf" by John Betjeman from *Collected Poems*.

Library of Congress Cataloging-in-Publication Data

Updike, John.
Golf dreams : writings on golf / by John Updike.—1st ed.
p.   cm.
ISBN 0-679-45058-0 (Knopf).—ISBN 0-449-22554-2 (Fawcett)
1. Golf—Literary collections. I. Title.
PS3571.P4G65   1996
813'.54 — dc20   96-4634
                                                  CIP

Manufactured in the United States of America
First Edition

Acknowledgments

Grateful acknowledgment is made to the following magazines and publishers, who first printed the pieces specified:

THE NEW YORKER: "Golf Dreams," "Drinking from a Cup Made Cinchy," "Is There Life After Golf?" "The Pro," "Intercession," "Farrell's Caddie," "Upon Winning One's Flight in the Senior Four-Ball."

GOLF DIGEST: "Swing Thoughts," "Those Three- or Four-Footers" (incorporating parts of "Putting Thoughts"), "The Gimme Game," "The Trouble with a Caddie," "Moral Exercise," "The Big Bad Boom," "The Camaraderie of Golf—I and II (II under the title "Golf Partner, Why Do I Love Thee?"), "Is Life Too Short for Golf?," "December Golf."

THE NEW YORK TIMES BOOK REVIEW: "Tips on a Trip."

ONTARIO REVIEW: "The Golf Course Proprietor."

MEETINGS & CONVENTIONS: "Golf as a Game of the People."

THE NEW REPUBLIC: "Golfers."

AMATEUR CHAMPIONSHIP ANNUAL: "The Bliss of Golf."

THE GOLF CLUB: "Golf in Writing" (developed from an afterword to *The Mystery of Golf,* by Arnold Haultain, reprinted by The Classics of Golf).

USGA 1988 OPEN PROGRAM: "Television Golf."

Acknowledgments

THE MASSACHUSETTS GOLFER: "Memoirs of a Marshal."
USGA 1984 WOMEN'S OPEN PROGRAM: "Women's Work."
SENIOR GOLFER: "The Yankee Golfer."

"Three Rounds with Rabbit Angstrom" and "A Good Round
with Tom Marshfield" are taken from the novels *Rabbit, Run,
Rabbit at Rest*, and *A Month of Sundays* (Alfred A. Knopf, Inc.).

For playing partners departed—Dorothy Wilde, John Conley, Ted Lucas, Miné Crane, Jerry Mason, Hank Bourneuf—and for those still swinging: Wick Potter, Ted Vrettos, Vas Vrettos, Steve Bergman, Dick Purinton, Josiah Welch, Joan Hart, Dick Harte, Jacques de Spoelberch, Arthur O'Brien, Peter Connolly, Sonny Palmer, Sid Cohen, Stuart Strong, Bill Nichols, David Updike, and Michael Updike, to mention but a few

Contents

Contents

LOVING THE GAME

Preface

THE VERY SUMMER in which I at last, acting on an old suggestion of my genial publisher, settled to the task of collecting my scattered pieces about golf turned out to be an unhappy one for my game. I don't know what went wrong. Simple aging, could it have been? For a number of years I have been nagged by an article by Gary Player in which he emphatically stated that golfers as they age *must* learn to draw the ball. I have always been, alas, something of a fader. A high straight ball was the best I could do. But then I came upon a tip from one of the female pros on how to draw the ball: you face the club toward the center of the fairway but swing as if for the right edge. It worked well during a few vacation rounds in Florida, with only my wife as witness, but turned out to be, in the slowly thawing North, before less sympathetic witnesses, a recipe for disaster. I began to hit just the top fraction of the ball, producing eighty-yard worm-burners off the tee and fairway woods of maximum futility and inconvenience. The errancy spread to my whole bag: I was blading soft

approaches clear across the green, hitting irons everywhere but on the sweet spot, and looking up even on
putts. I had lost the ability to turn in scores that warranted
my modest eighteen-handicap, and in my midnight de-
spair I would jot down, like lists of old girlfriends many
years married to some other guy, tips that had once
worked for me, e.g.:

1. loose grip
2. right elbow close to body
3. back in one piece
4. swing slow
5. begin downswing with left heel
6. keep the wrist-cock
7. don't try to "swish"
8. don't look up
9. think *"schwooo"*

Even when my game wasn't totally ugly, it lacked the *je
ne sais quoi* of yesteryear. The concluding hole at my home
course is a pretty, shortish par-four which on my good
days I played with a drive and then, say, a 7-iron that just
floated over the deep transverse bunker in front of the
green. I hit a good drive—my best of the day—and measured myself as ten yards inside the 150-yard marker. A
soft wind stirred in my face and, to be sure to clear the
bunker, I took a 5-iron, my club for the 150 distance. The
fairway lie was sidehill, with the ball a bit above my feet; I
caught it sweet, I thought. My playing partner said, while
the black dot was in mid-air, heading dead at the pin,
"What a lovely shot!" But, as he and I watched, instead of
bouncing on the green, the ball continued its descent on
down into the bunker. I was short. I couldn't hit a 5-iron

a lousy 140 yards. Earlier this summer, I had been examined by a new doctor, my doctor of four decades having at last retired, though he was scarcely older than I. The new doctor's nurse had me hop in my stocking feet on the scale to be weighed and measured. "Five eleven and a half," she said and, seeing the look on my face, asked with polite concern, "That sound right?" All of my adult life I had been measured at six feet. No more, no less. My image of myself was that of a six-foot man who could hit a 5-iron 150 yards. In all dimensions, *I was shrinking.*

My love of golf had been of its generous measurements—its momentary amplification of myself within a realm larger than life. If my golf was to shrink, as I had seen it shrink for others, to a mingy, pokey business of arthritic shoulder-turns and low, hippity-hopping drives that merely nibbled at the yardage, I would rather not tee up. Rereading these pieces, the oldest of them dating to 1958, has had, then, for me a bitter flavor of the valedictory. Beneath their comedy of complaints there ran always a bubbling undercurrent of hope, of a tomorrow when the skies would be utterly blue and the swing equally pure. But the *it* that Rabbit Angstrom discovers in the first of his matches described herein, the soaring grandeur that blooms of its own out of a good swing, now seemed one more youthful vision gone glimmering. My romance with golf stood revealed as hopeless. My arms were too long, my temperament too impatient, my sense of alignment too askew. From my golf dreams I had at last awoken.

As the summer dragged on, through what seemed an endless succession of obligatory matches, the suspicion crept over me that golf had stolen my life away: the hard gemlike flame with which I, as an artist, should have burned had been dampened if not doused by the green mists of this narcotic pastime. The fine edge that other penmen had dulled with whiskey and doses of Hollywood I had let rust into dullness while woolgathering over pronation and weight shift, wrist-cock and knee-bend. In the sluggish midst of a crowded member-guest tournament that had us waiting on nearly every shot, behind a foursome that putted with Solomonic deliberation, it occurred to me that, although I could not quite regret the time—the hours adding up to years of *temps perdu*—that I had spent playing the game myself, I certainly did resent the time I had devoted to watching other men play. Their fussy preparations, their predictable expostulations, the somehow sheepish smugness with which they repeated a crookedly grooved swing and the exact same errors that had dogged their golf for decades—how could I ever have thought this was a kind of paradise? Clearly, it was a hell faithfully answering Dante's description: circles of sinners frozen forever into an earned, ungainly agony. Perambulating these circles this hellish summer (in which there was never a dark cloud, a merciful rainout), I competitively met, now and then, men whose addiction had served to give them sound, repeating, victory-bent swings, and as they smilingly shellacked me and whatever partner I had incriminated in my criminal ineptitude I could take the measure of what price their excellence had extracted: total obsession, cruelly neglected wives and loved ones, business careers abandoned at the first opportunity, every non-golfing thought and consideration crowded to the parched margins of their cerebral cortices. I had balked at paying that price; I had betrayed golf's jealous god by trying to find fun and success elsewhere, by spreading my bets. And now I was suffering for it. "So then, because thou art lukewarm, and neither cold nor hot, I will spew thee out of my mouth": Revelation 3:16, for advanced beginners.

These thirty written evidences of an impassioned but imperfect devotion were composed in a variety of genres and appeared in a variety of places, some as deep in the literary rough as the Murdoch magazine *Meetings & Conventions* and *The Massachusetts Golfer.* Beginning in 1984, *Golf Digest* began to run an annual contribution from my starkly amateur point of view. Various tournament programs (the U.S. Amateur Championship in 1982, the USGA Women's Open in 1984, the USGA Open in 1988) invited me to contribute a little something and, flattered, I did. *The New Yorker* over the years accepted a number of golf-minded *jeux d'esprit,* and its editor the late William Shawn, with his uncanny omniscience, plucked from the torrent of books begging for his magazine's attention an authentic golf gem, Michael Murphy's *Golf in the Kingdom,* and gave it to me to review. From my fiction I have selected stories and scenes that bore especially upon the game, including three fraught rounds with Harry Angstrom, but not including some other vignettes, such as the choice opening segment of the short story "Deaths of Distant Friends." My longest article on golf, an account of the 1979 Masters for *Golf* magazine, I have omitted, as too newsy and outdated—it can be found in my collection *Hugging the Shore.* *Picked-Up Pieces* preserves another obsolete account, of a fancied lunar tournament following upon Alan Shepard's famous 6-iron shot on the moon in

1971. The dates in this book's table of contents signify the year of writing, which was usually also the year of publication. Twelve of the items between these covers have already appeared in other books of mine, and I would feel guiltier about that if I did not imagine that the ideal reader of *Golf Dreams* has been too busy perfecting his or her swing to be wallowing in my oeuvre.

J.U.

Learning the Game

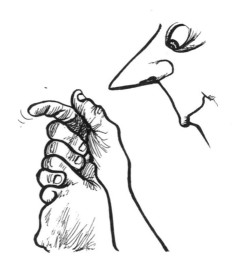

GOLF DREAMS

THEY STEAL upon the sleeping mind while winter steals upon the landscape, sealing the inviting cups beneath sheets of ice, cloaking the contours of the fairway in snow.

I am standing on a well-grassed tee with my customary summer foursome, whose visages yet have something shifting and elusive about them. I am getting set to drive; the fairway before me is a slight dogleg right, very tightly lined with trees, mostly conifers. As I waggle and lift my head to survey once more the intended line of flight, further complications have been imposed: the air above the fairway has been interwoven with the vines and wooden crosspieces of an arbor, presumably grape, and the land seems to drop away no longer with a natural slope but in nicely hedged terraces. Nevertheless, I accept the multiplying difficulties calmly, and try to allow for them in my swing, which is intently contemplated but never achieved, for I awake with the club at its apogee, waiting for my left side to pull it through and to send the ball toward that bluish speck of openness beyond the vines, between the all but merged forests.

It is a feature of dream golf that the shot never decreases in difficulty but instead from instant to instant melts, as it were, into deeper hardship. A ball, for instance, lying at what the dreaming golfer gauges to be a 7-iron distance from the green, has become, while he glanced away, cylindrical in shape—a roll of coins in a paper wrapper, or a plastic bottle of pills. Nevertheless, he swings, and as he swings he realizes that the club in his hands bears a rubber tip, a little red-rubber tab the color of a crutch tip, but limp. The rubber flips negligibly across the cylindrical "ball," which meanwhile appears to be sinking into a small trough having to do, no doubt, with the sprinkler system. Yet, most oddly, the dreamer surrenders not a particle of hope of making the shot. In this instance, indeed, I seem to recall making, on my second or third swing, crisp contact, and striding in the direction of the presumed flight with a springy, expectant sensation.

After all, are these nightmares any worse than the "real" drive that skips off the toe of the club, strikes the prism-shaped tee marker, and is swallowed by weeds some twenty yards *behind* the horrified driver? Or the magical impotence of an utter whiff? Or the bizarre physical comedy of a soaring slice that strikes the one telephone wire strung across three hundred acres? The golfer is so habituated to humiliation that his dreaming mind never offers any protest of implausibility. Whereas dream life, we are told, is a therapeutic caricature, seamy side out, of real life, dream golf is simply golf played on another course. We chip from glass tables onto moving stairways; we swing in a straitjacket, through masses of cobweb, and awake not with any sense of unjust hazard but only with a regret that the round can never be completed, and that one of our phantasmal companions has kept the scorecard in his pocket.

Even the fair companion sleeping beside us has had a golf dream, with a feminist slant. An ardent beginner, she confides at dawn, "I was playing with these men, I don't know who they were, and they kept using woods when we were on the green, so of course the balls would fly miles away, and then they had to hit all the way back. I thought to myself, *They aren't using the right club*, and I took my putter out and, of course, I kept *beat*ing them!"

"Didn't they see what you were doing, and adjust their strokes accordingly?"

"No, they didn't seem to *get* it, and I wasn't going to tell them. I kept *win*ning, and it was *won*derful," she insists.

We gaze at each other across the white pillows, in the morning light filtered through icicles, and realize we were only dreaming. Our common green hunger begins to gnaw afresh, insatiable.

DRINKING FROM A CUP
MADE CINCHY

(After Reading Too Many Books on How to Play Golf)

IN MY TOURS around the nation I am frequently asked, "Have you *ever* broken a cup?" Of course I have. Don't let anybody kid you on that score. *Everyone* who regularly drinks from china, no matter how adept he has become, has had his share of ruined tablecloths and scalded knees. *No human being* is born with the ability to take liquid from a cup successfully; you can easily prove this by trying to feed a baby. Those of us who have attained some proficiency have done so at the price of long hours of systematic application. Without these long hours our natural grace and poise would never have evolved into *skill*. I would not say that everyone is endowed equally; I *do* say that everyone, no matter how clumsy, can reduce his accidents to a minimum that will amaze his wife and friends. He can do this by rigorously adhering to a few simple principles that I have discovered through painful trial-and-error. Had these principles been available in legible form when I was young, my present eminence would have been attained by me *years ago*.

Drinking from a Cup Made Cinchy

I have analyzed drinking from a cup into three three-part stages: (1) Receipt, (2) The Cooling Pause, and (3) Consummation. However, bear in mind that in practice these "compartments" are run together in one fluid, harmonious social action.

I. Receipt

(1) Address the cup by sitting erect, your chest at right angles to the extended arm of the cup-offerer, or "hostess." Even if this person is a spouse or close relative, do not take a relaxed, slouching position, with the frontal plane of your rib cage related obliquely to the cup's line of approach. Such an attitude, no matter how good-naturedly it is assumed, has the inevitable effect of making one of your arms feel shorter than the other, a hopeless handicap at this crucial juncture, where 30 percent of common errors occur. The reason: *both hands should move toward the saucer simultaneously.*

(2) In seizure, first touch, with feathery lightness, the rim of the saucer with the pad of the index finger of the right hand. (Left-handers: read all these sentences backward.) A split-second—perhaps .07—later, the first knuckle of the middle, "big" finger, sliding toward the center of the saucer's invisible underside, and the tip of the thumb *must* coördinate in a prehensile "pinching" motion. *This motion must occur.* The two remaining fingers of the right hand of necessity accompany the big finger, but should not immediately exert pressure, despite their deep-seated instinct to do so. Rather, the wrist is gently supinated. This brings the two passive fingers into contact with the underside of the saucer while at the same time

the cup is drawn in toward the body by a firm, but not angry, forearm.

Meanwhile, the left hand is not just "taking Sunday off." Fingers and thumb united in one scooplike unit (an imaginary line drawn through the knuckles should intersect your foot), the left hand hovers, convex without being "balled" into a fist, an inch or two (whichever feels most natural) to the left of the inner left edge of the saucer. What is it doing there? Many beginners, having asked this question and failing to receive an adequate answer, keep their left hands in their pockets and fancy that they are achieving insouciance. They are not. They are just being foolish. The left hand, in its "escort" role, performs many functions. For one thing, its close proximity to the right hand gives that hand confidence and eases its fear. For another, the index and middle fingers are now in a position to swoop over and hush the distressing but frequent phenomenon of "cup chatter," should it develop. Thirdly, if the spoon, with its eccentric center of gravity, begins to slither from the saucer, the left hand is there to act as a trap. Fourthly, if worse comes to worst and the cup tips, the left hand can rush right in and make the best of a bad situation, whose further ramifications take us into the psychological realm discussed in the chapter "To Err Is Human."

Throughout, keep your eyes travelling rapidly around the rim of the cup.

(3) The saucer is held by your right hand, the "executor." Your left hand, the "guardian angel," cruises in the air inches away. A napkin—the "landing field"—has been previously spread on your right knee. *Now* softly *constrict.*

By this I mean, with one impulse, bring your forearms in toward your sides, bend your spine forward, bow your head, and touch your knees. Without any thought on your part, this syndrome of actions will lead the cup and saucer to descend along a parabolic line whose equation on Cartesian coördinates is $2x = y^2$. At $x = 0$, the tea will be on your knee. Your left hand will have automatically joined the right *under the saucer* and as automatically glided away. You will find that your thighs have become firm flat surfaces. For the first time since your index fingertip touched the icy edge of china, you may smile.

II. The Cooling Pause

(1) The key to this phase—in point of time the longest of the three—is *immobility*. Only the fingers, eyelids, and tongue move at all. Resolutely maintain your bent position over the cup. Think of yourself as "mothering" the beverage. Let your stillness be placid, vegetal, and Olympian, rather than rigid, electric, and Byzantine. Be diffident and amiable in conversation. Some of my fellow pros advise beginners not to speak at all, but such total exclusion is apt to be in itself unsettling. However, *do* avoid anecdotes requiring much facial or other animation, and arguments whose logical structure must be indicated by any action of the hands, whether in drawing diagrams in the air or ticking off points on the fingers.

(2) Resist the temptation, once the saucer appears secure, of straightening up in the chair (or, worse, sofa), thereby placing a long diagonal hypotenuse between your nose and the cup. Any hauteur is felt *throughout the body.*

Dignity of bearing is *no substitute* for muscular control. An obsequious, attentive hunch will not be thought rude as long as you are able to raise your eyes to your hostess fitfully. Indeed, the distention of the eyebrows needed to glimpse her lends to many people an arch charm of mien they otherwise would lack.

(3) Rotate the broad part of the spoon—*not* the handle—in the liquid. Do not splash. Do not toy with the fascinating ripples individual droplets make. Do not attempt to return liquid from the saucer to the cup. *Be still.*

III. Consummation

"My goodness," I can hear many readers asking, "will we never get a taste of the brew?"

"Yes, you will" is my answer—"especially if you have followed my advice up to now." The reason I have outlined the procedure so meticulously is this: having come thus far without a blunder, you feel "clean" and possess the crispness to go on. Success succeeds. If I am wrong, see the chapter titled "There's Many a Slip."

(1) Steam has ceased to arise from the liquid and you are certain it is cool enough to drink. Restore the spoon to the saucer, pinning it with the left thumb. Look around and make sure no one is about to jostle you, either in fun or by accident. The physical action of bringing food to the mouth is so ancient, so fundamental to Man, that a detailed description would be mere padding. The one ticklish procedure that remains is the Separation of Cup and Saucer.

(2) The two possible extremes—leaving the saucer on

the knee or bringing it with the cup all the way to the chin—are too contemptible to denounce, though I have seen both done. In fact, the problem is self-solving if, contrary to instinct, you pick up the saucer with the *left* hand, gripping the cup handle with the right. They begin the ascent together, but the inequality of their strengths soon tells; in the powerful yet delicate grasp of the right hand, the cup completes its flight to the lips, while the left hand weakly halts at the level of the sternum, where the saucer, braced against your necktie, acts as a tacit bib.

(3) Be conscious that, as you consume the beverage, the weight of the cup diminishes; otherwise the right hand may snap it clear over your shoulder. Never hang on to an empty cup. *Get rid of it.* In replacing the unit on the table or tray presumably provided, a jaunty clatter need not be avoided, if it can be induced without force. When your hands are at last free, sigh and say, "That was delicious," or "I needed that."

Congratulations. You have just drunk from a cup.

Appendix: Helpful Hints

1. Don't be tense.
2. Don't be "loose."
3. Think of yourself not as an assembly of hinged joints inflexibly connected by rods of calcium but as a plastic, pliant animal, capable of warmth, wit, and aspiration.
4. Think of the cup-and-saucer complex, from the instant it is received into your hands to the instant it leaves, as a charge delivered to your care and toward which you feel the maternal emotions mentioned above (II.1). Imag-

ine yourself "crooning" to it, recognizing hereditary re-
semblances to your own face in *its* face, etc.

5. The angle made by the forearms should *never* exceed
110 degrees or fall below 72 degrees, assuming the room
is at less than body temperature. If it is not, you need my
companion work, "The Elements of Sipping Through a
Straw."

TIPS ON A TRIP

I HAVE BEEN ASKED* to write about golf as a hobby. But of course golf is not a hobby. Hobbies take place in the cellar and smell of airplane glue. Nor is golf, though some men turn it into such, meant to be a profession or a pleasure. Indeed, few sights are more odious on the golf course than a sauntering, beered-up foursome obviously having a good time. Some golfers, we are told, enjoy the landscape; but properly the landscape shrivels and compresses into the grim, surrealistically vivid patch of grass directly under the golfer's eyes as he morosely walks toward where he thinks his ball might be. We should be conscious of no more grass, the old Scots adage goes, than will cover our own graves. If neither work nor play, if more pain than pleasure but not essentially either, what, then, can golf be? Luckily, a word newly coined rings on the blank Formica of the conundrum. Golf is a *trip*.

A non-chemical hallucinogen, golf breaks the human

---

*By *The New York Times Book Review*, in the summer of 1973.

body into components so strangely elongated and so tenuously linked, yet with anxious little bunches of hyperconsciousness and undue effort bulging here and there, along with rotating blind patches and a sort of cartilaginous euphoria—golf so transforms one's somatic sense, in short, that truth itself seems about to break through the exacerbated and as it were debunked fabric of mundane reality.

An exceedingly small ball is placed a large distance from one's face, and a silver wand curiously warped at one end is placed in one's hands. Additionally, one's head is set a-flitting with a swarm of dimly remembered "tips." Tommy Armour says to hit the ball with the right hand. Ben Hogan says to push off with the right foot. Arnold Palmer says keep your head still. Arnold Palmer has painted hands in his golf book. Gary Player says *don't* lift the left heel. There is a white circle around his heel. Dick Aultman says keep everything square, even your right foot to the line of flight. His book is full of beautiful pictures of straight lines lying along wrists like carpenter's rules on planed wood. Mindy Blake, in *his* golf book, says "square-to-square" is an evolutionary half-step on the way to a stance in which both feet are skewed toward the hole and at the extremity of the backswing the angle between the left arm and the line to the target is a mere fourteen degrees. Not fifteen degrees. Not thirteen degrees. Fourteen degrees. Jack Nicklaus, who is a big man, says you should stand up to the ball the way you'd stand around doing nothing in particular. Hogan and Player, who are small men, show a lot of strenuous arrows generating terrific torque at the hips. Player says pass the right shoulder under the chin. Somebody else says count two knuckles on the left hand at address. Somebody else says *no* knuckle should show. Which is to say nothing about knees, open or closed clubface at top of backswing, passive right side, "sitting down" to the ball, looking at the ball with the left eye—all of which are crucial.

This unpleasant paragraph above, strange to say, got me so excited I had to rush out into the yard and hit a few shots, even though it was pitch dark, and only the daffodils showed. Golf converts oddly well into words. Wodehouse's golf stories delighted me years before I touched a club. The tales of Jones's Grand Slam and Vardon's triumph over J. H. Taylor at Muirfield in 1896 and Palmer's catching Mike Souchak at Cherry Hills in 1960 are always enthralling—as is, indeed, the anecdote of the most abject duffer. For example:

Once, my head buzzing with a mess of anatomical and aeronautical information that was not relating to the golf balls I was hitting, I went to a pro and had a lesson. Put your weight on the right heel, the man told me, and then the left foot. "That's all?" I asked. "That's all," he said. "What about the wrists pronating?" I asked. "What about the angle of shoulder-plane vis-à-vis that of hip-plane?" "Forget them," he said. Ironically, then, in order to demonstrate to him the folly of his command (much as the Six Hundred rode into the valley of Death),* I obeyed. The ball clicked into the air, soared straight as a string, and fell

---

*"Forward, the Light Brigade!"
  Was there a man dismay'd?
  Not tho' the soldier knew
    Someone had blundered:
  Theirs not to make reply,
  Theirs not to reason why,

Theirs but to do and die.
Into the valley of death
  Rode the six hundred.

     —ALFRED, LORD TENNYSON,
  "The Charge of the Light Brigade"

in a distant ecstasy of backspin. For some weeks, harboring this absurd instruction, I went around golf courses like a giant, pounding out pars, humiliating my friends. But I never could identify with my new prowess; I couldn't *internalize* it. There was an immense semi-circular area, transparent, mysterious, anesthetized, above the monotonous weight-shift of my feet. All richness had fled the game. So gradually I went back on my lessons, ignored my feet, made a number of other studied adjustments, and restored my swing to its original, fascinating *terribilità*.

Like that golf story of mine? Let me tell you another: the greatest shot of my life. It was years ago, on a little dogleg left, downhill. Apple trees were in blossom. Or the maples were turning; I forget which. My drive was badly smothered, and after some painful wounded bounces found rest in the deep rough at the crook of the dogleg. My second shot, a 9-iron too tensely gripped, moved a great deal of grass. The third shot, a smoother swing with the knees nicely flexed, nudged the ball a good six feet out onto the fairway. The lie was downhill. The distance to the green was perhaps 210 yards at this point. I chose (of course) a 3-wood. The lie was not only downhill but sidehill. I tried to remember some tip about sidehill lies; it was either (1) play the ball farther forward from the center of the stance, with the stance more open, or (2) play the ball farther back, off a closed stance, or (3) some combination. I compromised by swinging with locked elbows and looking up quickly, to see how it turned out. A divot the size of an undershirt was taken some eighteen inches behind the ball. The ball moved a few puzzled inches. *Now here comes my great shot.* Perfectly demented by frustration, I swung as if the club were an ax with which I was reducing an orange crate to kindling wood. Emitting a sucking, oval sound, the astounded ball, smitten, soared far up the fairway, curling toward the fat part of the green with just the daintiest trace of a fade, hit once on the fringe, kicked smartly toward the flagstick, and stopped two feet from the cup. I sank the putt for what my partner justly termed a "remarkable six."

In this mystical experience, some deep golf revelation was doubtless offered me, but I have never been able to grasp it, or to duplicate the shot. In fact, the only two golf tips I have found consistently useful are these. One (from Jack Nicklaus): on long putts, think of yourself putting the ball half the distance and having it roll the rest of the way. Two (from I forget—the comic strip *Mac Divot?*): on chip shots, to keep from underhitting, imagine yourself throwing the ball to the green with the right hand.

Otherwise, though once in a while a 7-iron rips off the clubface with that pleasant tearing sound, as if pulling a zipper in space, and falls toward the hole like a raindrop down a well; or a drive draws sweetly with the bend of the fairway and disappears, still rolling, far beyond the applauding sprinkler, these things happen in spite of me, and not because of me. On the golf course as nowhere else, the tyranny of causality is suspended, and life is like a dream.

THE PRO

I AM on my four-hundred-and-twelfth golf lesson, and my drives still have that pushed little tail, and my irons still take the divot on the wrong side of the ball. My pro is a big gloomy sun-browned man—age about thirty-eight, weight around 195. When he holds a club in his gloved hand and swishes it nervously (the nervousness comes over him after the first twenty minutes of our lesson), he makes it look light as a feather, a straw, a baton. Once I sneaked his 3-wood from his bag, and the head weighed more than a cannonball. "Easy does it, Mr. Wallace," he says to me. My name is not Wallace, but he smooths his clients toward one generic, acceptable name. I call him Dave.

"Easy does it, Mr. Wallace," he says. "That ball is not going anywhere by itself, so what's your hurry?"

"I want to clobber the bastard," I say. It took me two hundred lessons to attain this pitch of frankness.

"You dipped again," he tells me, without passion. "That

right shoulder of yours dipped, and your knees locked, you were so anxious. Ride those knees, Mr. Wallace."

"I can't. I keep thinking about my wrists. I'm afraid I won't pronate them."

This is meant to be a joke, but he doesn't smile. "Ride those knees, Mr. Wallace. Forget your wrists. Look." He takes my 5-iron into his hands, a sight so thrilling it knocks the breath out of me. It is like, in the movies we all saw as children (oh, blessed childhood!), the instant when King Kong, or the gigantic Cyclops, lifts the beautiful blonde, who has blessedly fainted, over his head, and she becomes utterly weightless, a thing of sheer air and vision and pathos. I love it, I feel half-sick with pleasure, when he lifts my club, and want to tell him so, but I can't. After four hundred and eleven lessons, I still repress.

"The hands can't *help* but be right," he says, "if the *knees* are right." He twitches the club, so casually I think he is brushing a bee from the ball's surface. There is an innocent click; the ball whizzes into the air and rises along a line as straight as the edge of a steel ruler, hangs at its remote apogee for a moment of meditation, and settles like a snowflake twenty yards beyond the shagging caddie.

"Gorgeous, Dave," I say, with an affectation of camaraderie, though my stomach is a sour churning of adoration and dread.

He says, "A little fat, but that's the idea. Did you see me grunt and strain?"

"No, Dave." This is our litany.

"Did you see me jerk my head, or freeze at the top of the backswing, or rock forward on my toes?"

"No, Dave, no."

"Well then, what's the problem? Step up and show me how."

I assume my stance, and take back the club, low, slowly; at the top, my eyes fog over, and my joints dip and swirl like barn swallows. I swing. There is a fruitless commotion of dust and rubber at my feet. "Smothered it," I say promptly. After enough lessons, the terminology becomes second nature. The whole process, as I understand it, is essentially one of self-analysis. The pro is merely a catalyst, a random sample, I have read somewhere, from the grab bag of humanity.

He insists on wearing a droll porkpie hat from which his heavy brown figure somehow downflows; his sloping shoulders, his hanging arms, his faintly pendulous belly, and his bent knees all tend toward his shoes, which are ideally natty—solid as bricks, black and white, with baroque stitching, frilled kilties, and spikes as neat as alligator teeth. He looks at me almost with interest. His grass-green irises are tiny, whittled by years of concentrating on the ball. "Loosen up," he tells me. I love it, I clench with gratitude, when he deigns to be directive. "Take a few practice swings, Mr. Wallace. You looked like a rusty mechanical man on that one. Listen. Golf is an effortless game."

"Maybe I have no aptitude," I say, giggling, blushing, hoping to deflect him with the humility bit.

He is not deflected. Stolidly he says, "Your swing is sweet. When it's there." Thus he uplifts me and crushes me from phrase to phrase. "You're blocking yourself out," he goes on. "You're not open to your own potential. You're not, as we say, *free*."

"I know, I know. That's why I'm taking all these expensive lessons."

"Swing, Mr. Wallace. Show me your swing."

I swing, and feel the impurities like bubbles and warps in glass: hurried backswing, too much right hand at impact, failure to finish high.

The pro strips off his glove. "Come over to the eighteenth green." I think we are going to practice chipping (a restricted but relaxed pendulum motion) for the fiftieth time, but he says, "Lie down."

The green is firm yet springy. The grounds crew has done a fine job watering this summer, through that long dry spell. Not since childhood have I lain this way, on sweet flat grass, looking up into a tree, branch above branch, each leaf distinct in its generic shape, as when, in elementary school, we used to press them between wax paper. The tree is a sugar maple. For all the times I have tried to hit around it, I never noticed its species before. In the fall, its dried-up leaves have to be brushed from the line of every putt. This spring, when the branches were tracery dusted with a golden budding, I punched a 9-iron right through the crown and salvaged a double bogey.

Behind and above me, the pro's voice is mellower than I remember it, with a lulling grittiness, like undissolved sugar in tea. He says, "Mr. Wallace, tell me what you're thinking about when you freeze at the top of your backswing."

"I'm thinking about my shot. I see it sailing dead on the pin, hitting six feet short, taking a bite with lots of backspin, and dribbling into the cup. The crowd goes *ooh* and cheers."

"Who's in the crowd? Anybody you know personally?"

"No . . . wait. There *is* somebody. My mother. She has one of those cardboard periscope things and shouts out, 'Gorgeous, Billy!' "

"She calls you Billy."

"That's my name, Dave. William, Willy, Billy, Bill. Let's cut out this Mr. Wallace routine. You call me Bill, I'll call you Dave." He is much easier to talk to, the pro, without the sight of his powerful passionless gloom, his hands (one bare, one gloved) making a mockery of the club's weight.

"Anybody else you know? Wife? Kids?"

"No, my wife's had to take the babysitter home. Most of the kids are at camp."

"What else do you see up there at the top of the backswing?"

"I see myself quitting lessons." It was out, *whiz*, before I had time to censor. Silence reigns in the leafy dome above me. A sparrow is hopping from branch to branch, like a pencil point going from number to number in those children's puzzles we all used to do.

At last the pro grunts, which, as I said, he never does. "The last time you were out, Mr. Wallace, what did you shoot?"

"You mean the last time I kept count?"

"Mm."

"A hundred eight. But that was with some lucky putts."

"Mm. Better stand up. Any prolonged pressure, the green may get a fungus. This bent grass is hell to maintain." When I stand, he studies me, chuckles, and says to an invisible attendant, "A hundred eight, with a hot putter yet, and he wants to quit lessons."

I beg, "Not quit forever—just for a vacation. Let me play a few different courses. You know, get out into the world. Maybe even try a public course. Gee, or go to a driving range and whack out a bucket of balls. You know, learn to live with the game I've got. Enjoy life."

His noble impassivity is invested with a shimmering, twinkling humorousness; his leathery face softens toward a smile, and the trace of a dimple is discovered in his cheek. "Golf is life," he says softly, and his green eyes expand, "and life is lessons," and the humps of his brown muscles merge with the hillocks and swales of the course, whose red flags prick the farthest horizon, and whose dimmest sand traps are indistinguishable from galaxies. I see that he is right, as always, absolutely; there is no life, no world, beyond the golf course—just an infinite and terrible falling off. "If I don't give *you* lessons," the pro is going on, "how will I pay for *my* lessons?"

"*You* take lessons?"

"Sure. I hook under pressure. Like Palmer. I'm too strong. Any rough on the left, there I am. You don't have that problem, with your nice pushy slice."

"You mean there's a sense," I ask, scarcely daring, "in which *you* need *me?*"

He puts his hand on my shoulder, the hand pale from wearing the glove, and I become a feather at the touch, all air and ease. "Mr. Wallace," he says, "I've learned a lot from your sweet swing. I hate it when, like now, the half-hour's up."

"Next Tuesday, eleven-thirty?"

Solemnly my pro nods. "We'll smooth out your chipping. Here in the shade."

SWING THOUGHTS

"Hɪᴛ ɪᴛ with the back of your left hand" was the first swing thought I ever heard, brusquely but not unlovingly put to me by the aunt-in-law who had moments before placed a golf club in my virgin grip. I was twenty-five, and had spent my youth in a cloistered precinct of the middle class where golf was a rumored something, like champagne breakfasts and divorce, that the rich did. Not only had I never held a golf club before, I had never thought about the back of my left hand before. I thought hard about it and took a murderous divot out of my aunt-in-law's lawn.

Well, there was clearly great charm and worth in a sport so quaintly perverse in its basic instructions. Hit down to make the ball rise. Swing easy to make it go far. Finish high to make it go straight. I read Arnold Palmer, who said to think of my feet and head as the three apexes of an immovable triangle; your feet should feel like bricks, was one of his tips, with no indication of how your head should feel. Jack Nicklaus put great store in a little rightward cock of his head at takeaway, so his left eyeball and the golf ball were inexorably aligned. Gary Player preferred to think of a core of metal passing up through the middle of his body; he twisted around it like a barbecued chicken on an upright spit. Hale Irwin has lately said he thinks of his hands and the club handle riding down an imaginary flume of water. Sam Snead thinks of waltz time, or of spanking the ball on its backside; his arms, he says, feel like ropes as he swings. Lee Trevino on television recently said to accelerate the back of the left hand through the ball toward the target—which puts me back where I began thirty bedevilled years ago.

I write, without doubt, as a poor golfer, who came to the game late, with frazzled eye-hand connections. But there are millions like me, shanking and topping away in a happy fog—"golf," after all, is just "flog" spelled backward—so my thoughts on swing thoughts may bring a little light into that outer darkness surrounding the televised championships where phlegmatic blond boys drill 4-irons two hundred yards dead to the pin.

The basic duffer flaw is anxiety, which leads him to hit from the top, too fast and with too much right hand (in the case of a right-handed golfer). He is afraid of letting go of the earth, so he keeps his weight on the right leg and his knees prudently locked. He is afraid of the result, so he looks up, lifting his head that fatal microsecond too soon and hitting the ball as if with a flyswatter or hoe. Any swing thought that restrains these anxious tendencies is a good one; a thought that has usually worked for me, though for whole summers I have forgotten to think it, is *Begin the downswing as slowly as possible.* This serves to keep the head set over the ball and discourages that right elbow from leaping out from the side to give the club a counterproductive extra push. It also affords the weight shift time to occur and delays the uncocking of the wrists. Any number of inner advisements serve the same end: beginning the downswing as if pulling on a rope, imagining that the club is falling from the top, beginning with a tug or a slide of the left hip toward the target. Anything to keep those anxious hands from jumping down at the ball.

The right elbow is anxiety's henchman; the tips intended to keep it close to the body are legion. Herbert Warren Wind writes of the great Joyce Wethered's right elbow seeming to brush her side on the downswing. *Don't chicken-wing it,* an old playing partner used to say to me. The trouble is, since there really is time for only two thoughts in the course of a two-second golf swing, we don't want to waste one of them on a negativity and a basically trivial section of the anatomy. In general I have had poor long-term luck with swing thoughts involving odd bits of the body, such as *Glide your right knee toward the hole,* or *Pass first one shoulder under your chin and then the other,* or *Rest your right ear on an imaginary pillow at the finish.* These things should happen, but thinking about them leaves the arms and hands free to do too much mischief, and emphasizes our anxious sensation of being a rickety assembly of parts, any one of which might go awry.

This same old friend also would say, *Throw your hands at the hole,* which, reckless as it sounds, does get the hands in front of the moving clubhead and does, if the grip isn't twisting, send the ball toward the hole. Once the swing is commenced, a second thought must keep it going, for only a full swing *through the ball* produces a sweet result. A Gestalt approach translates the unnatural complications of the golf swing into some instinctive motion. We all can *throw* a club without thinking, with the proper weight-shift; one sparkling afternoon I was hitting string-straight boomers by imagining that I was throwing the driver down through the ball, toward the hole. The next day that I tried it, though, I kept hitting a foot behind the tee.

For a time I had success forgetting my body entirely and concentrating on the image of the clubface striking the ball; picturing the face of a wedge nicely brings your hands and weight forward and usually averts a skull. But such a fine focus has a way of creating constraint in a situation already fraught with constraints; the ideal swing thought liberates the golfing body from its trepidations into a certain relaxed largeness of free motion. *Turn your back* was a simple directive that, when I remembered it, at least packed some torque into the top of the swing. *You are a rubber man*, I used to say to myself—not a man of rubber bands but of something hardish yet springy, like a rubber tire. Or, transcending anatomy entirely, I would think of the course as a succession not of narrow fairways and perilously rimmed greens but of generous depressions, great receptive areas that I only had to hit broadly "in the direction of" to obtain success. With fairway woods this worked especially well.

The difficulty is, all swing thoughts decay, like radium. What burned up the course on Wednesday has turned to lead on Sunday. Yet it does not do to have a blank mind: the terrible hugeness of the course will rush into the vacuum and the ball will spray like a thing berserk. A swing thought is the golfer's equivalent of the rock climber's

Don't look down. With a particular focus we reduce the huge circumambient room for error to a manageable somatic radius. The score, the stakes, the beers in the clubhouse should all be ousted by *some* swing thought—which is a swing thought in itself.

THOSE THREE- OR FOUR-FOOTERS

THE 1994 SEASON of network golf began with an unexpected duel between two sturdy ghosts from the 1970s, Johnny Miller and Tom Watson, vying to win the AT&T Classic, formerly the Crosby Invitational. Watson, looking happily at home in the blustery winds of Pebble Beach (where he had won his last Open), appeared to have it sewn up, with a two-stroke lead and four holes to play. But on both the sixteenth and seventeenth he managed to putt too far past the hole and missed the three- or four-footer coming back. Miller, whose own putting was not unshaky, parred in and won by one.

Viewers could certainly empathize with Watson's travail. How often, needing only to two-putt to cement a triumph, have we managed to do the same! On the lag, the ball rolls bravely at the hole, misses narrowly, and then—oh, no!—slides on and on, beyond tap-in range, beyond gimme range. Our opponents and playing partner maintain an ominous silence as we briskly, manfully stride up to the "eminently makable" short putt; we affect a debonair little half-smile as if to say, "Nothing to it." But the butterflies in the stomach have hatched, and as we take our stance the line of the putt wriggles and slips around like a snake on glass. We somehow can't see it. If the putt were shorter, we would ram it at the back of the cup; longer, and the break of the green would be obvious. But at this maddening in-between length all systems break down. Typically, we decide to aim at the right edge, hit it a tad too firm, and watch it in sickening slow motion catch the right edge and twirl out, while our partner suppresses a groan and our opponents exchange a silent wink. Or, correcting for this scenario, we go for the dead middle, hit the ball a bit tentatively, and see it wobble off to the left in the last six inches.

Golf is rarely more hateful than at such moments. We wish we were dead, or at least safe at the office, where a man gets some respect. A sliced or hooked drive has a certain grandeur, a chunked iron shot can be grimly chased down the fairway and struck again, and a foozled chip has its gentle comedy. But there is nothing funny or grand about an easy putt that declined to roll into the hole, especially when the match, as in the Watson-Miller case, hinged on it. No athletic excuse will do; the test was purely of our nerve and judgment, and the test was failed.

Well, maybe it wasn't an easy putt. The only putts that are easy are the ones that top off a triple bogey and have already been conceded. Perhaps a secret to the pressure-laden three- or four-footers is to imagine that they *have* been conceded and we are putting them purely for the practice. Certainly some days they present no problem: the line is clear, the stroke is simplicity itself. When we go astray, as a general rule, we are outsmarting ourselves—

specifically, we are allowing for too much break. Unless the lie on the green is steeply sidehill, an edge of the hole is probably as divergent a target as you need. Don't give the hole away. The putt should be firm enough to go a foot past, and it can be helpful to forget that the target is a hole at all; I have had good luck, some days, imagining that I am trying to hit a matchbox or cigarette pack set up on the near lip.

Seeing is a crucial part of putting, and too rarely discussed is the crucial matter of what, exactly, the putting person should be looking at. Bobby Locke, considered by many the greatest of them all at this abstruse art, advises looking at the *back* of the ball, as if one were driving a tack into it; in my experience this produces a crisp, on-line stroke but often too hard a one. One feels "back"—an inch farther away from the target. For years, following a tip of Jack Nicklaus's, I used to pick a fleck of grass an inch or two in *front* of the ball, and try to roll the ball over it; this produced pretty good feel and direction but meant, unsettlingly, that I wasn't quite looking at what I was hitting. Some days I picture a right triangle, with my left foot, bearing most of my weight, set on one leg of it, the putter going back along the other, and the ball poised at the apex, ready to be stroked along, as it were, the extended longer leg. This sounds complicated but gets the weight on the correct foot and moves the ball along a line.

Putting is the sick man of golf, as we can see from the extremity of some of the applied remedies: Bernhard Langer switch-hitting and clamping his right forearm to the club shaft with his left hand, Ken Green crouching over his son's twenty-two-inch baby putter, and Bob Lohr putting one-handed. I once played with a man who firmed

up his putter head behind the ball and then hit while looking at the hole; it worked quite well for him, but thoroughly spooked the rest of us, as if we were playing with
a staring zombie.

Visualization is key: a putt we can't picture is almost
never going to drop. But what a picture, what a Cubist
tangle, we are trying to paint, in three dimensions that
shift axis every time we move our heads! If only we had
frog's eyes and could see the ball and the hole at once!
Bending our gaze to the white orb, we forget where the
hole just was; it jiggles around in the memory like a star
twinkling through smog, while the green seems to sway
like the deck of a rolling ship. It helps, I have found, on lags
especially, to think of the trimmed earth beneath one's
feet—immobile, two-dimensional—and to project one's
mind down into a ball travelling along this surface. To *become* the ball, in some sense, on its little linear journey.

An eighteen-inch putt is in full view—ball, cup, and the
line between. But with a putt longer than that, the hole
disappears from peripheral vision, and three- or four-
footers can be missed because the golfer, subconsciously
trying to widen his field of vision, moves his head. Make
a mental image of the line and then keep your head as still
as if on a fifty-foot lag. Suppress also the wider horizons
entailed by such thoughts as *If only I hadn't charged that
putt*, or *If only I had remembered that the grain slopes toward
the sea*, or *If I miss this we will be the opposite of dormie, whatever that is*, or *If I miss this Johnny Miller will win the tournament and get all those headlines and exemptions*. . . . Golf
must be played one stroke at a time. One *unhurried* stroke
at a time; in our impatience to see the result, we tend to

stab at short putts, in one anxious, self-defeating motion. As much as a drive, a putt is formed of two parts: back and forward, with a pause between.

Hold the putter lightly, so it can impart momentum and direction out of its gentle swing; follow through as far as you took it back. Having determined the line through visualization, hit the ball as if it's a straight putt, letting the break take care of itself. Try to feel the clubhead moving close to the turf, and the ball hugging this same surface in its gravity-bound flight. Challenge yourself with the notion that this putt *should* be made; bogey-shooters sink into a lazy two-putt fatalism that leads to three-putts.

These smooth advisements come readily to my pen but, putter in hand, I tend to choke. Standing with one's eyeballs hanging five feet above a dimpled sphere the same size is a dizzying experience. Once, caught in a foursome with three heavyweight golfers on the stately layout of the Country Club in Brookline, I managed, in the pinch, to miss a putt no longer than a tall man's shoe. It didn't even touch the cup. It was, my playing partner amiably told me on the way to the next tee, "the goddamnedest worst putt" that he had ever seen.

"It's a game of inches," was all I could tell him.

Choking is one aspect of golf that, from the start, came naturally to me. Given even a paper-thin opportunity to let my side down and destroy my own score, I will seize it. "It's all on you, partner!" is a sure-fire battle-cry to swing extra hard and dribble the ball into the flowering weeds. The muttered hint, "Remember, you have a stroke here," freezes my joints like a blast from Siberia.

My best rounds tend to come when I am playing with just one other person, whom I have known a long time;

the competition is simple and friendly, and it's easier to maintain a rhythm. In a foursome, I do best if my partner is steady and excellent, and if our opponents are physically handicapped in some way. Bad backs, arthritic knees and hands, emphysema, newly bought bifocals, and sand that has worked in behind contact lenses are among the afflictions in others that give me a sense of strength and ease, and that enable me to swing, as Sam Snead advises, at eighty-five percent of my strength. Anything like a fair and even match, I try to swing at a hundred five percent. Golf is one sport where a rush of adrenaline does more harm than good, producing, at the professional level, approach shots that fly the green and approach putts that hurry past the hole. Johnny Miller, interviewed after his victory at the AT&T, seemed dazed and amused, and said that all day he hadn't believed he could win it. Watson may have been revved up by the thought that he could.

As the 1994 season continued, the pros continued to demonstrate that those pesky three- or four-footers are not easy. This same Tom Watson's creditable run at the British Open went glimmering when several putts of this length slid by. Helen Alfredsson wasted her early lead at the U.S. Women's Open with a remarkable barrage of such misses, including that familiar horror, a downhill three- or four-footer that became *another* three- or four-footer, also missed. If, at the professional level, sinking ten- and twelve-footers is what makes birdies, sinking three- or four-footers is what staves off bogeys. At every level, missing enough of them turns a fair day sour, and a good round bad.

THE GIMME GAME

THE PURPOSE OF A GIMME, as I understand it, is to save golfers the time and effort it takes to make a tap-in and then bend over (this is the hard part) and pull the ball out of the hole. That's fine. But when does a tap-in become a missable putt? Even a putt of two inches can be whiffed, pros such as Hale Irwin have demonstrated,* and certainly a sidehill one-footer on a slippery green is no cinch. "Within the leather" used to be the standard, when all putters had leather handles and were much the same length. What I detect now, in the rough-and-ready foursomes I play with a trio of conniving thieves, is the erosion of every standard by the creeping assumption that *all* putts are, construably, gimmes.

Case A: Mr. Black, lying three, makes a rather shabby approach putt that settles a good stride from the hole. If he sinks it, it will be a five. His partner, Mr. White, sinks

---

*At Birkdale, during the British Open, in 1983. He went on to lose by one shot.

a four-footer for a five. Mr. Black announces, "So this doesn't matter," and knocks his putt away, scoring himself for a five.

Case B: On the next hole, Mr. Blue, of the opposing pair, putts up to within two feet. Sinking it would make four, to tie Mr. Black. He looks up winsomely and says, "We gave you one longer than this on the previous hole." Mr. Black, enlisting in a conspiracy of generosity, says, "Go ahead, pick it up." Thus Mr. Blue pars the hole.

Case C: The next hole is a battle of bogeys. The Black-White team has their five. Mr. Green, lying three, asks his partner, Blue, to putt out for a tying bogey and then charges his par putt for the win. When it races six feet past the hole, he gives himself that putt, since of course if he wasn't fighting for a team victory he would have lagged it up for a cinch five.

Case D: Mr. White has a twenty-incher for a win. With a visible uncertainty, in the surrounding silence, he steps up quickly, half-heartedly stabs at the ball, watches it slide past, and brazenly announces, "Hey, I wasn't really trying. I assumed it was a gimme. *Ob*viously it was a gimme. Here, I'll do it again, this time for real. See? I couldn't miss."

Case E: Black and Blue, tied, have putts of three to four feet. Black says to Blue invitingly, "Good-good?" Black's putt is a few inches longer, but Blue figures that if Black sinks it the pressure on his own putt will have doubled. It will become a must putt. If he misses, Black and White will laugh and Green will groan. "Good," Mr. Blue agrees, and he and Black pick up.

And so it goes in this match, with everyone too good-humored and gentlemanly not to concede anything inside the span of a kangaroo's leap, and any putt not critical to the scoring, however lengthy, waived away. So a mentally adroit golfer in obliging company can go eighteen holes without actually sinking a single one of those shortish white-knuckle character-builders that the pros, we see on television, miss more than occasionally. Of course, they are playing for hundreds of thousands and we are playing for a dollar a side. Still, aren't we depriving ourselves of one of golf's satisfactions—the rattle of the ball incontestably dropping into the cup for an honest if humble score?

I confess that I have gotten so caught up in the gimme game that, rather than risk missing a four-footer, I have asked my partner to putt out so that I could slap my own now-meaningless putt triumphantly away. I have even inwardly prayed that my opponent sink his long putt so that the testing one in front of me would no longer matter. *I want my putts not to matter* becomes the bottom line, and if this isn't the formula for golf gutlessness and the crunchtime yips, then Jack Nicklaus never won a major. When local tournament time comes, and the opponents are not Blue and Green but big-swinging Mr. True and golf-lawyer Mr. Mean, the golfer grown soft on concessionary golf will wilt like plucked lettuce in sunshine. A simple silence surrounding the usual dimpled gimme will strike him as a personal insult and hostile challenge; his emotions in a turmoil, his eyeballs in a swivet, he may well choke and miss, and thus plunge himself headlong into an afternoon of humiliation and misdirected adrenaline. Adrenaline, properly directed, eats putts up—the tasty, measured mental picturing of the line, the firm yet judicious stroke along the first inch of that line, the momen-

tary union of ball and grain and slope, the hungry gulp of
the swallowing cup.

So, easy on the gimmes, friends. I try not to accept the
gift of any putt that in my heart I know I might miss. If I
don't miss, the satisfaction is worth the lumbar twinge of
bending down to retrieve the ball from its little oubliette.
If I do miss, well, that's the game—the *real* game. Golf's
scoring is so bracingly rudimentary it seems a pity to nib-
ble at its edges and eliminate the delicate passages played
on the shortest grass, with a gentle finesse reminiscent of
pool, croquet, and marbles. The strokes you save with
a sheaf of gimmes are there to haunt you when reality
moves back in. But what, you say, of the valuable minutes
that conscientious putting adds to golf's already extensive
playing time? Well, if it's time you're wanting to save, stay
off the course entirely, and show up at the clubhouse only
to turn in the scores you might have had if every stroke
were a mulligan, a free drop, or a gimme.

THE TROUBLE WITH A CADDIE

A CAMPAIGN IS AFOOT to bring back the caddie to American golf courses. In *Golf Digest* and elsewhere you can read of the many benefits: It is better for the aging golfer's cardiovascular system to walk than to ride, better for the course not to have motorized carts flattening the grass into shiny highways of dying turf, better for the caddie himself to be lugging two twenty-pound bags than flipping cholesterol-rich hamburgers at McDonald's. Furthermore, the pros do it. Where would Lee Trevino be without jolly Herman Mitchell handing him his trusty wedge, or Nick Faldo without the beautiful albeit hefty Fanny Sunesson murmuring sweet nothings into his ear as they crouch together over the line of a putt? What is a more swankily *golfy* feeling than swaggering unencumbered down the fairway with your clubs tagging along on the shoulder of a stout, freckle-faced lad? Arriving at the gleaming ball, the two of you hold a brief, mutually respectful consultation from which emerges a 6-iron lovingly polished to a rare lustre by the lad's ministrations with a damp towel as he strolled in your wake. Then, while this youngster falls into a worshipful silence, you keenly eye the distant green, take a thoughtful waggle or two, and, to the music of a profoundly rhythmic *swish* and *click*, swing. "Oh, bravely struck, sir!" the caddie cries, in near-ecstasy. "But for the excessive backspin you imparted to the ball, it would verily have popped into the cup!"

Idyllic though this vision is, some caddie-resistance persists, at least within me. Basically, I want to be alone with my golf. I don't mind my partner and opponents being there—without them, there is no game, just practice—but to have a couple of youthful (usually) strangers also in attendance turns the game into a mob sport. My golf is so delicate, so tenuously wired together with silent inward prayers, exhortations, and unstable visualizations, that the sheer pressure of an additional pair of eyes crumbles the whole rickety structure into rubble. *What is the caddie thinking?* keeps running through my mind, to the exclusion of all else. And, *How he must hate me!* Or perhaps, with that last foozled 3-wood, I have passed into a netherworld beneath his contempt. My wish to please the fellow, or at least to stop sending him on futile searches in the woods and the wild-raspberry thickets, where the toxins of poison ivy and Lyme tick disease assault his bare shins, becomes obsessive and counterproductive, one of golf's magic maxims being that, the harder you try, the worse you play.

Come, man, snap out of it, I can hear the caddie-advocates snorting—*it's all in your mind.* Yes, but that is just where golf is played, in the mind. *You are being oversensitive and narcissistic: your caddie doesn't care how well or badly you are playing.* Well, if he doesn't care, why is he following me like a shadow, grunting every time I top the ball? *We mean,* the caddie-advocates might riposte, *that he doesn't care to the extent that you should tense up. He wishes you well, but in a detachedly friendly, non-involved way; for him this is just a job.* You said it. Golf for me is meant to be play, if not bliss, and here is this kid making it feel like a job, a job from which I should be fired for flagrant incompetence.

The fact is, most Americans are uneasy with servants. In our democratic fashion we keep thinking of them as people. The French nobles were surrounded by servants through every detail of their morning toilette; this was possible because the servants weren't people, they were human artifacts, constructed to serve. Not that golf is quite as private an activity as the morning toilette, but it is toward the intimate end of the continuum, somewhere between making love and writing a poem. Imagine writing a poem with a sweating, worried-looking boy handing you a different pencil at the end of every word. My golf, you may say, is no poem; nevertheless, I keep wanting it to be one—a series of effortless sweet shots engraved on the air, with some crisply tapped putts for punctuation. There is an inner space in which this fabulation must be shaped. Some banter tossed to an old buddy across the fairway doesn't violate the space, but the gatheringly real personality of a caddie, as he breathes down your neck, does.

Of the last caddie in my experience, I learned, as we strode along together, that (a) he had a degree in business administration and was looking for a job in the depressed Massachusetts market, (b) he had been up until three-thirty the night before, drinking, (c) his girl friend had once read one of my books, (d) he wanted me and my partner to win the match so he could carry our bags for another day of the tournament and "make the moola," (e) he expected to receive rather more in payment than the posted fees declared. When I mentioned the twenty dollars a round that was the official charge, he couldn't suppress a laugh right in my face. So, in addition to my golf worries, I had to shoulder concern over his job prospects, his state of fatigue and hangover, his girl friend's literary life, and his tip.

Indeed, the caddie's tip, approaching as inexorably as one's own death, and sooner, becomes a ruinous preoccupation. I have never had a caddie over fourteen years of age who did not look disgruntled when he was paid. Under fourteen, they are still financially innocent, and grateful for anything green. But in Ireland, once, after a round in a gale that mixed snow with a driving rain, I saw a pack of snarling caddies turn and attack the leader of our golf tour, who stuck to his proposed gratuity at the risk of his life. The caddies in Scotland and Ireland are not preambling their career; this *is* their career, pursued day after plodding day under a dark cloud of Celtic stoicism and alcoholic vapors. Standing downwind from one is enough to make your putter wobble. Their intricate expertise often seems gratuitous: they tell you a ball is lost while it's still in the air, and that a forty-foot putt will break an inch to the left at the end. They bet among themselves, evidently, on the outcome of the matches they are caddying for, and some of their advice may be deliberately counterproductive. Nevertheless, a hard-won wisdom lurks in those crinkly eyes that have smilingly watched so many visiting Yank and Japanese foursomes come to bitter grief in the venerable bunkers and grassy dunes. All an American caddie's eyes hold is the glaze of a childhood spent staring at a television set. At first, he gives you an 8-iron for 150 yards, as if you are Fred Couples; by the end of the round, he is handing you a 3-iron and telling you to punch it.

Will the back-to-caddies movement succeed, and will its ecological benefits make up for the loss of the Amazonian rain forest? Or will it fail, and those delightfully humming little golf carts, which never expect a tip or emit a snicker, reduce every course between Pebble Beach and Shinnecock Hills to rutted desert? Keep tuned to this station. In my case, until my knees buckle I will carry my own bag; golf is one misery that doesn't necessarily love company.

MORAL EXERCISE

LET US ASSUME that most of the men and women with the
leisure and wherewithal to play seriously at golf have attained in their lives a somewhat cushioned position. The
executive hears mostly acquiescent words from his inferi-
ors; the judge judges others; the retired actress receives
rave reviews from her maid and her third husband. Most
of us (to include a sexagenarian writer in this cushioned
category) don't really know how well we're doing, in real
life, and imagine we're doing not so bad. The world con-
spires to flatter us; only golf trusts us with a cruelly honest report on our performance. Only on the golf course is
the feedback instantaneous and unrelenting—the ball
cannot be browbeat out of the place in the poison ivy
where we placed it, or euphemized up from the water into
which it just so sickeningly plonked. A putt that rims the
cup is definitely not in, no matter what you write on your
scorecard. The game and your swing provide a barrage of
criticism that there is no evading. What other four hours'
activity can chasten a magnate with so rich a variety of

disappointments, or unman a lothario with so many re-buffed desires? Golf is a square shooter. In the sound of the hit and the flight of the ball it tells us unflinchingly how we are doing, and we are rarely doing well.

We cannot hide from golf behind a plea of physical lim-itations. We will never outjump Michael Jordan, or out-rally Monica Seles, but we have all, if we have played a few years, hit some perfect golf shots. Not as far as John Daly, perhaps, but right up the middle, or right on the pin, or right into the cup. The ball whistled off the grooves and bit on the green with backspin, or else bounded down the fairway with overspin. And it felt effortless. So, why not do this every time? Since we have demonstrated the phys-ical capability, the reason must be characterological. Our bad golf testifies, we cannot help feeling, to our being bad people—bad to the core. Socrates or his mouthpiece Plato thought that to know the good was to do the good, automatically. But, like a character out of Dostoevsky, we perversely continue to play with wild and self-punishing imperfection.

For instance, two persistent faults of duffers are hitting from the top and looking up. Both are the product of un-reasonable anxieties: the fear, in the first instance, that the ball will go away if we wait a split-second longer, and, in the second, that it will get lost if we keep our head down. The results are hideous: hundreds of foozled, smothered, topped, sliced, and shanked shots. Experience tells us, over and over, that the clubhead gathers ideal speed from quiet hands and passive arms and a slow start out of the backswing, and that taking your eye off the ball destroys the contact; and yet our primitive intuitions and appetites, when the adrenaline flows, overrule painfully acquired wisdom. Unreconstituted Adam wants to kill the ball, and to watch it fly. We lack the mustard-seed of faith that keeps the swing smooth and the parts of the harmonizing body all in place.

The correct golf swing is a web of small articles of faith, all of which strain common sense. To squat slightly to the ball, with flexed knees, feels unnatural; it feels like a weakening of the strength stiff legs impart. Taking a light grip goes dead against our furious determination to hammer the course into submission. The takeaway, low to the ground and to the inside, violates our native-American impulse to lift the club up and straight back and to tomahawk the ball into the next county. And the all-important weight-shift, whether conceived of as a push of the right foot, a twitch of the left hip, or a downward pull, as of a bell-rope, with the straight left arm, feels as if we are throwing our bodies off a cliff, into thin air. No, thanks. We would rather keep our weight solidly planted on the right foot, well away from the edge of the cliff, and with a labored scoop of the arms pull that ball twenty degrees to the left.

One learns rather little watching the pros on television—they make it look too easy, like gravity-defying computer graphics—but earlier this year I admired a culminating shot of Tom Kite's, in the Atlanta Classic. He had won only one tournament in nearly two years, and was said to be over the hill, but now he had a two-shot edge. His drive was sitting up in the short rough on the righthand side of the fairway of the eighteenth hole, a par-five with water here and there. He was on national television. He should have been as tight as a tin man left out in the rain; even a pro would have been forgiven for playing up short, chipping on, and taking his winning par. But no: with that ghostly little half-smile of his, Kite plucked a wood out of the bag—a 4-wood, I think—and whipped through the ball with a swing that left the club hanging down his back and his back foot up on its toe like a ballerina's in its little pink slipper. It was picture-book fluidity, and the ball landed not only on the green 220 yards away but close enough for him to sink the putt and finish with a superfluous, superlative eagle. A lifetime of tournaments, and a certain undying joy in the game, had gone into that marvellous trust in his swing, that saintly *letting go* that golf asks of its devotees.

Most of us cannot let go and let the genie out of the lamp. We know he's in there, hidden in our bones and muscles, because he does emerge now and then. When he does, we wind up asking him for ten more yards on the drives, and he goes back in. Golf is a study in our greed as well as our lack of faith. In remembering a round, we write off the missed two-foot putt and the approach shot that just barely drifted into the trap as not us, as not legitimately part of the round, but incorporate without gratitude the skulled wedge that somehow wound up on the green, and the drive that bounced off the out-of-bounds stake back into the middle of the fairway. In the heat of the round, on the narrow thirteenth with your partner out of the hole, you stand watching your hooked 7-iron vanish into the woods with the burning conviction that it wasn't you who just hit that shot: it was, instead, an imposter, a demon, an alien from outer space who momentarily breezed into your body. But it *was* you, and facing this disagreeable fact is one of the moral lessons of golf. Another is to yield up, within the framework of sound swing principles, hope of utter control; the free swing produces the straight shot.

Golf morality runs to paradoxes. He who hits down sees the ball soar. He who looks up tops the ball into the tall grass. He who tries to hit hardest loses yardage to the supple devil-may-care. He who strives to steer the ball into the hole winds up stubbing the putt. "He who would save his life must lose it," a rabbi once advised. "Let the nothingness into yer shots," the imaginary pro Shivas Irons instructed his disciple in Michael Murphy's lovely *Golf in the Kingdom.* Don't try too hard, we might more simply say. Or: seize the day. Golf's ultimate moral instruction directs us to find within ourselves a pivotal center of enjoyment: relax into a rhythm that fits the hills and swales, and play the shot at hand—not the last one, or the next one, but the one at your feet, in the poison ivy, where you put it.

Playing the Game

INTERCESSION

This short story was written early in my golf career. The remote innocence of the time may be read not only in the sub-dollar greens fee but in the surreal presence of three solo golfers— "onesomes"—spaced out on a public course. As in the golf scene in Rabbit, Run, *written a year or so later, the eerie religious latency and hallucinatory trickiness of the milieu is stressed; like Rabbit, my young hero is partnered with an irritating alter ego, and has some growing up to do. But to any beginning golfer, miracles, rarely benign, abound.*

THE DROUGHT THAT HAD FALLEN on all Connecticut that summer fostered illusions. In the burned landscape of orange grass, the little red flags were hard to see, and the watered putting greens seemed hallucinatory ponds. Workmen were straightening the road nearby; rose-colored dust from the construction drifted across the first fairway. A road builder tried to wave Paul on. Paul shifted into second by way of defiance and racily cut in front of a truck bearing a pointed hill of blue spalls and continued in this loud gear a distance up the road that was not being improved.

He parked the car well over on the shoulder and lifted the borrowed bag of clubs from the back seat by the strap, inexpertly, so that the weight of their heads nearly spilled the clubs into the weeds that grew at the edge of the right of way. He was new to the game of golf in all its aspects. His wife's uncle had initiated him less than two weeks ago. On most of the days since, Paul had dutifully spent some time batting hollow, perforated practice balls back and forth on his own lawn. Their stunted flight was, very quickly, unsatisfying. You could not improve beyond a point; half the shots went straight, humming a little, and the rest dribbled off obliquely. Only on a golf course, with real distances and solid balls, could his prowess be measured. Nevertheless his wife had looked amazed when, after lunch, he threw her uncle's clubs into the car and left her alone with the house and child. He wrote the plot of a syndicated adventure strip, so she was used to having him home all day.

Inside a white clapboard shed, one entire side of which was painted with the figures *85¢*, an old fat dark woman sat brooding like a prophetess, and a bin of soft drinks gave off with peculiar pungency the chemical odor of refrigeration. "You're alone," she told Paul, and sold him a scorecard and pencil. Above her head hung stroboscopic posters of Gene Sarazan and Dr. Cary Middlecoff. On another wall a gray cardboard chart demonstrated the progress of a defunct tournament. By the light of this sibyl's eyes Paul suddenly felt that the shape of his heart was clumsily visible, as if behind bathroom glass. Doing anything in public for the first time—carving a roast, taking communion, buying a tuxedo—made the front wall of his chest feel fragile and thin. He didn't dare ask her where the first tee was; he left the shed and walked uncertainly around it.

As he emerged from behind the far corner a man not five yards away checked his swing and stared. Apologetically humpbacked, Paul scuttled, with a bobble of clubs, across the man's line of drive and took a place obsequiously far behind him. The man was freckled and iron-haired, except for red eyebrows; these stood out from his forehead like car-door handles. The gray hair furring the back of his neck in tiny controlled tufts led without sharp transition into a fuzzy cap, tactfully checkered, Scots in accent, its visor too short to shade his eyes except at noon. With one gloved and one bare hand he gripped a beautifully pale wood. Paul wondered what made sandy men so smug. Blond women were the same; these Paul could pardon, but not this old fop. With a swing as lucid and calm as the legendary perfect circle that Giotto in one brush stroke drew to win a commission, the Scotsman sent the ball deep into the fairway, within easy chipping of the green. His face was vacant, his soul flying with the ball. Then, so gently he might have been hooding a falcon, he fitted the golden head of his club with a chamois cover, and replaced the club in a bag on wheels, and pulled this cart after himself.

Paul took some considered swings at the puff of a dandelion. A potent repose, he imagined, was building in him. As the distant Scotsman took his iron shot, Paul planted a white tee in the patch of clay. When he straightened up, a tall kid with bony brown arms was standing close by. Though he had not noticed the boy before, Paul promptly said, "I guess you're ahead of me."

"I believe so." The niceness of the boy's diction combined oddly with his basketball sneakers.

"O.K. Go ahead."

"Shall we go around together?"

Paul was flattered to think that the boy had mistaken him for near his own age. He was greedy about looking young; at twenty-six, he looked twenty-three and wanted to look eighteen. "Thanks a lot, but you'd better go ahead. I'm pretty lousy."

Paul expected the protests an adult would have made, but the boy simply believed him, saying, "All right," with a monkeyish nod. "Thank you." The front of his T-shirt, bearing the faded name of Alsace High School, hung as limp as wash from his shoulders. He turned to business; his arms above the elbow seemed no wider than the bone. With a huge loose swing the kid sliced the ball high over the road, the workmen, and the cloud of pink dust, into the yard of a stucco house. "They can keep it," he announced sneeringly to nobody and teed up again. This time, he both hooked and topped; the ball streamed through the green grass near a watering hose, began to bounce rapidly when it hit a scorched area, and leaped a narrow drainage ditch. Paul regretted that he had not accepted the invitation. The kid, huffing indignantly through his nose, fetched yet another ball from the pocket of his bag. His third try went straight and far.

"Couldn't be better," Paul offered.

"Yes, it could." The kid smiled at him with an unaccountable condescension, considering the performance he had just put on. "But I will accept it."

"That's good of you."

"What?"

"Nothing."

Still, Paul was so annoyed that, when his turn finally came, he pressed. The ball followed the route of the kid's second try: through the grass to his left, over the ditch, into the second fairway, which lay parallel to the first, going the other way. The elegant Scotsman was poised on the second tee. As Paul crossed over he could see the tiny figure against the trees check his swing.

Playing alone did not make for calmness. Rather, the lack of any witness but the sun's steady eye induced panic. Paul hurried, though there was no one behind him. He left lost balls lying in the underbrush and impatiently picked up disgraceful putts. He felt guilty, guilty about the most innocent things—about leaving his wife alone in the house for a few hours, about not working all day long like other men, about having grown up at all and married and left his parents alone together in Ohio, about being all by himself in this great kingdom of withered turf. The very volumes of air insecurely fenced by the multiple shifting horizons of the rolling course seemed freighted with guilt, pressing his ball down, making it fly crazy. His progress across the course became a jumbled rout. The fourth hole asked that you clear a tangled dry marsh, and the fifth, attacked from a tee that was a rubber mat beneath a plum tree, was out of sight over a crest, where the grass, never shaded, had turned a desolate salmon color and matted into the dirt. A weathered pink flag marked the place to aim at. Walking after his mediocre drive, he noticed, thirty yards to his right, a second pink flag, and when he descended into the shallow valley where the putting green had been laid, the flag in the hole said 7. He had skipped two holes. The approach to 5 had been to his right, and the approach to 6 must be intertwined somewhere, perhaps behind those spruces. The high-school kid, hitting a different ball at every third stride, was coming up *behind* him. "How're you doing?" he called.

"Awful," Paul answered.

"Stupid," the boy said to his ball as it skipped off the far edge of the green. He dropped another at his feet and swung more gingerly, with better success. He dropped a third and came within inches of the cup. "You *better* get wise," he told it.

Caught between the kid and the Scotsman, Paul had to keep going. The backs of his calves ached. His left thumb threatened to blister, and squinting into the sun had pinched his forehead. Paul didn't expect his body to turn querulous; not long ago it had accompanied him without complaint on any exertion, as forgiving and tireless as a dog at his heels. The Scotsman was setting out from the ninth tee, a little ziggurat by an elm. Paul slumped to the bench there. He glanced skyward to measure the day and noticed, on gauzy cirrus clouds near the sun, the explicable but eerie phenomenon of iridescence—a faint circular rainbow. The distant machines constructing the road made, all together, a squeaking, cranking noise.

The kid joined him. "What's your score?"

"I haven't kept it. I can't count that high."

"I never keep score on the first nine. My father told me, Don't bother. Just concentrate on getting tuned in. That's what I do." He whirled a club around and stared Byronically into an apple tree. "Do you know how many holes of golf I play every day? How many do you guess?"

"Six," Paul said.

"Forty-five or even fifty-four. One day I played seventy-two. How many do you play usually?"

"Hardly any. I just started. These aren't even my clubs—I borrowed them."

"Want to go around the next nine with me?"

The quaint precision of the boy's diction, which was what Paul remembered most vividly of his earlier invitation, had relaxed somewhat. His chubby tanned face, cheerful and fat-lipped below the eyes, was betrayed by the nervously moist brown eyes, and the prominent cupped ears. Studying the boy, Paul's eyes became those of another kid, and he recognized that his companion was generally disliked. At that age, braggarts always are, but they don't know how to stop. Paul had been stupid to see nothing unhappy in a youngster playing golf by himself all day like a retired banker. The boy's home, a glance at his glossy new clubs confirmed, was prosperous and fond, the type whose chaste, conceited, unpopular children poke around libraries and luncheonettes and have hobbies intensely and never quite hear the drum.

"Sure," Paul said, "but I warn you—I'm really poor." He wondered about the boy's age. Height told nothing any more. Paul guessed fifteen at the oldest; his elbows were so broad, and he was so bluntly eager to go first, so sure it was an advantage.

The kid stared down at the ninth green, which seemed shorter than the two hundred yards advertised. "I have to be careful," the kid said. "I usually overshoot this one."

But, though he tried twice, he did not. "Well," he pronounced, "not *too* rotten. See if *you* can get on."

Paul laughed; such frank competition tickled him. This age was so grainy, so coarse. How coarse he did not remember until he sliced his ball into an apple tree and was unable to find it among the fallen fruit. The kid found it for him and shouted, "Boy, do you have great eyesight!" and, pinching his nostrils, cried for the world to hear, "Peeyew!"

Together they returned to the first tee. Paul had decided the secret was to make believe he was swinging at a hollow ball, casually, in his own yard. Though his drive was less good than the kid's, his approach was close, and he chipped on in three. By this time, the kid had several balls to play. Relieved at his fair showing, Paul felt friendly enough to confess, "Now, if I could putt I'd have a par. But I can't putt."

"Let's see you."

"It's your honor. I'm closer."

"Go ahead. I want to see you put the ball right in. What's your grip?"

"It's nothing. Just a grip."

"O.K. now, just swing naturally. You're less than six feet away. A stinking baby could do it blindfolded."

Tense, Paul pushed too weakly, and the slant of the green dragged the ball off to the right.

"Look," the kid said, "be natural. You know how I putt? I'm just natural." He scrunched into an arabesque and, his hands braced against his belt, switched the club awkwardly. "And then just naturally put it in," he said, "bingo, like that. Look at me. I just step up to the ball"—Paul's now. "I'm not *afraid*. I just look at the hole, take a natural grip, and . . . bingo!"

As the kid led the way over a path through trees that were, with the heat and the insects, already starting to drop leaves, he said, "I got two fours on that hole. What did you get?"

"I suppose five. You sank my putt for me."

"We'll call it a five."

"If I'd sunk my own putt, I'd have had a four," Paul said.

"You want to hear some of my scores? Thirty-three on one round. Thirty-five another time. Seventy-two and seventy-three on one day, one in the morning and one in the afternoon. You know how long I've been playing? Guess."

"Seven years," Paul said.

"Eleven days."

"Really? You're very good, for eleven days."

"I like the game," the kid said. "I don't like it as much as fishing, but next to fishing I guess I like it best."

"You like fishing? Isn't it dull?"

"Dull, listen—there isn't a sport you can say that less of."

"Is it a sport? I think of a sport as taking skill and fishing just a lot of sitting," Paul said.

"Trout fishing? Are you kidding? Marlin fishing? Listen, there's nothing more skillful, believe me. Ted Williams is the most skillful baseball batter there is, and he's only a fair fisherman."

"I thought he was pretty good."

"Yeah. That's what the sportswriters say."

"Well, he probably isn't much good at shot-putting, either," Paul said.

"There's no comparison between those two things."

They crossed a little wooden bridge and came to the second tee. Paul asked, "Who goes first?"

"You can. Go ahead."

"Oh, no, you don't. It's your honor. You got two fours and I only got a feeble five."

"Go ahead. I want to study your swing."

To the right of the tee, for perhaps a city block, were woods. Paul arranged his hands, squeezed, bent his left knee, inhaled, and kept his eye so intently on the sphere of dimpled rubber that the intervening air seemed to petrify. Like a bird escaping, his swing fluttered through his hands. The mathematics of the parts had felt perfect, yet, in sum, the drive sliced into the woods, ricocheting forever into the frothy green depths.

"You know what you do? You use your wrists too much. Use your arms. Here—let me see your grip. Is *that* it? Ugh. Now what's your thumb doing all the way over *here?* You going to be a contortionist or something when you grow up? Look how I hold it—natural. Be natural. Who taught you to stick your thumb down there? You're going to get a blister."

"My wife's uncle said, to keep the face of the club from turning." The fact was out: he had a wife. A little freeze of surprise did perhaps catch at the kid's features for a second, but immediately he recovered and went on the attack again.

"Who's her uncle? A golf pro?"

"No, he just plays a lot."

"Boy, all these people with their crackpot systems. You listen to all of them, you'll go nuts. My *father*, and a guy he plays with who's pretty near a pro, he's as good as a pro, he was second in a tournament three years ago that was nearly statewide—*they* say just take a natural grip and pay no attention to everybody's weird systems." He teed up and said, "Swing nice and easy, with your arms pretty stiff. Like this." But the double load of talking and showing was too much for him, and his ball, topped, skittered thirty yards down the burnt-out fairway. He turned and said to Paul, "That's your way. This is *my* way." His second drive was beautiful and long. "Now. Which way is better, your way or my way?"

"Your way."

"O.K." With a touching clownish grin, the kid bowed from the waist. "Never argue with Professor Shaw."

"All right," Paul said. "Which is better: your way"—he pointed into the woods, where he had driven his first ball—"or *my* way?" Paul had primitive faith; he really believed that, having thus committed himself, he would be rescued. During the moment after impact it seemed true, for the connection had felt solid, but while they watched, the ball, high as an airplane and piloted from within, curved more and more to the left and finally fell on the bank of ragweed and thistle near the road. The workmen had gone, their day done.

Professor Shaw said, "That's *good?*" and walked off down the center of the fairway, retrieving his topped ball on the way, without looking back. Perhaps Paul's having a wife had scared him after all.

Paul had expected him to ask, "What do you do?"

The answer would be, "I think up the plot for a comic strip called *Brace Larsen*."

The boy's face would be blank.

"One of the Hartford papers carries it."

"You just think up the story and let somebody else draw the pictures?"

Imagining this conversation while walking along with the dry grass in his eyes and the strap of the golf bag irritating his shoulder, Paul was losing patience. "That's right. I wanted to draw when I was a kid but the syndicate bought my ideas for this other guy to do up. They say anybody can execute; it's ideas that are rare."

Yet the boy's face would retain, clear as day, Paul's own conviction as a child that ideas were nothing and the actual drawing all that counted.

He was gone from the third tee when Paul reached it. It was a very short hole, 115 yards, backed by maples and flanked by fruit trees; the kid was walking toward the green, well to one side. Paul shouted, "Whajja get, Professor?" There was no answer. The strangeness of the illusion that the warps of the course had confronted him with himself of ten years ago had obscured the plain fact that he did not really like the kid—the fat-lipped, daddy-loving brat. To be patronized and then evaded by a minor offended Paul's dignity as taxpayer, as husband, as father of a daughter to whom he was half the world, and as the creator of a plot which appeared in seventy-eight newspapers including one in Hawaii. It struck him as especially unjust, this daily extension of himself halfway across the Pacific yoked to this childish snub. Too annoyed to arrange his feet, Paul swung a mashie powerfully and with a start of pride and alarm that swelled his throat saw the ball coming down right on top of the kid. "Jesus, look out!" he called. The boy turned and threw up an arm as if shielding his eyes from the sun, and remained in that pose some seconds. Either Paul's eyes lied or the ball passed right through his body. Heaven protected fools.

When he got there, Shaw was among the maples, looking. Dappled by shade, the planes of his face had the innocent frowning bluntness of an animal's.

Paul said, "Gee, I'm sorry. I damn near killed you."

"You didn't even come close. Boy, are you wild." Paul liked the idea of his being wild. It was a long-lost kind of companionship, poking around together in dead leaves and the roots of brush. "I got a three on each of the last two holes," Shaw announced pleasantly. "This might be one of my better rounds."

"That's *won*derful. Hey, you needn't bother to hunt. The thing only cost thirty-five cents."

"What was the name on it?"

"I don't know."

"Was it Wilson?"

"I don't know. I doubt it."

"I just found a Wilson. I guess it's mine if it's not yours. Was yours new?"

"Not terribly."

"This makes three I've found today. A lot of these rich guys, they don't even *bother*."

They searched a bit longer. Paul, certain that what the boy had pocketed was what he was looking for, angrily smashed at small green plants and split young saplings by bringing his club down on their fork.

"I give up," he said. "Let's go on. This leaves me one goddamn ball."

Professor Shaw glanced at him, somewhat offended by the swearing. "I can sell you a couple," he offered seriously. Paul disdained to answer.

At the fourth tee, the kid flubbed one into the marsh and teed up a second time and got across.

"If at first you don't succeed," Paul said, "try, try again."

"Huh?" He had, of course, heard. The boy's face went slack with such distinct fright that Paul momentarily relented, and addressed the ball. All he wanted was that his drive be perfect; it was very little to ask. If miracles, in this age of faint faith, could enter anywhere, it would be here, where the causal fabric was thinnest, in the quick collisions and abrupt deflections of a game. Paul drove high but crookedly over the treetops. It dismayed him to realize that the angle of a metal surface striking a rubber sphere counted for more with God than the keenest human hope.

"Boy, you'll never find that," the kid said. This time he didn't help Paul hunt. The ball must have landed in a breadth of desiccated swamp on the other side of the trees. The mud of the swamp, in drying, had cracked in neat rectangles; the weeds were filmed with dust that ballooned upward at a blow. As Paul circled, his ankles gathered burrs. His thumb hurt; his face burned with sun and shame. Panic added its own blush; it was late, he should be home, he had no business here, he must hurry. That had been his last ball. He floundered to the edge of the short grass, reaching for his wallet—he would buy a couple of balls from the kid—and saw a white speck yards away, high and clear on a brown slope. He was so sure he had played into the swamp that it was several seconds before the feeling of the ball's placement in space being miraculous wore off. He went up to it, and it was absolutely his own. A Maxfli with a smile in it. His faith surged back. He had outplayed the boy here; he was, when you came right down to it, the better golfer, being the older man, a resident of real life.

"I found it!" he called to Professor Shaw, who was walking past, on his way to the fifth tee.

"Why'd you bring it out so far?"

"I didn't bring it out. This is where it was. It cleared everything."

"I got another three on that hole."

"Well, who the hell *could*n't get a three if they took as many chances as you do? Hell, all you do is take about nine shots and then count the only three that are any good. If you played according to any rules, a stinking baby could beat you. *I* could beat you."

For the first time, the boy laughed; his teeth gleamed like the rims of two cups, but his averted eyes showed he had taken the wound. "I was demonstrating to you," he weakly said.

Now Paul laughed. "Look," he said. "I'll bet you a dollar a hole I can beat you. If you play according to the rules I'll put up a dollar of mine against a beat-up golf ball of yours on every hole. That's five dollars you can make. Holes five, six, seven, eight, and nine." He pulled out his wallet.

The boy was standing far enough away so that they had to shout across the intervening space; his image shimmied as a wave of heat came off the ground. His voice came: "Keep your money."

"You're afraid," Paul told him. "Rotten a player as I am, you know I'll beat you."

"No," the boy said in a strained voice and began walking.

"I'll catch up!" Paul shouted. "Easy money, Professor!"

He waved the wallet above his head, but the boy wouldn't look.

Paul chipped onto the green and hastily putted twice. On the fifth tee, beneath the plum tree, looking across toward the two pink flags, ivy red in the rays of the declining sun, Paul felt exalted and certain. The kid, a burnished and melancholy stick figure, passed in front of the far flag, and Paul aimed for the double image. Socked flatly, the ball floated for a great distance in a leftward sweep and never rose, it seemed, six feet off the ground. That he had hooked did not diminish his conviction that he was destined to give his opponent a deserved trouncing. The ball bounced once in the open and, as if a glass arm from Heaven had reached down and grabbed it, vanished. His eyes marked the exact spot in the air where it had disappeared.

He walked there. The scarcely sloping land where his ball should have been was unmarked by a bush or tree or ditch; on this table of stricken grass any hint of white would have glared. There was nothing. Heaven protected fools.

Hardly aware that he had made a decision, Paul shifted the bag of clubs on his aching shoulder and walked toward the road, where his dusty car waited. It was almost dinnertime; the little girl would be in the tub, gurgling in glee at Daddy's return.

He had never seen the fifth green of this little course, and inadvertently pictured it as paradisiacal—broadleaved trees, long-tailed birds, the cry of water. Professor Shaw might wonder why his new buddy failed to appear over the rise, but kids accept things easily; they haven't lived long enough to be sure of what's customary. Paul pictured himself at that age with disgust, as if holding a grub in his hand. The abandoned road-building machines stood among piles of dirt like beasts paleontologists had uncovered. In all the landscape no human being was visible, and a fatiguing curse seemed laid on everything. Damned game.

THREE ROUNDS
WITH RABBIT ANGSTROM

My four novels centered on Harry "Rabbit" Angstrom show the hero shifting his athletic passion from basketball to golf. In Rabbit, Run, *in the summer of 1959, he is re-introduced to the game (which he had encountered in boyhood, as a part-time caddie) by the Reverend Jack Eccles, an Episcopalian minister who seeks, with such friendly attentions, to win Rabbit back to Janice, the wife he has abandoned, from Ruth, the woman he is living with.*

THEY TURN OFF THE ROAD and go up the winding drive to the clubhouse, a big cinder-block building fronted with a long sign that has CHESTNUT GROVE GOLF COURSE lettered between two Coca-Cola insignia. When Harry caddied here it was just a clapboard shack holding a wood-burning stove and charts of old tournaments and two armchairs and a counter for candy bars and golf balls you fished out of the swamp and that Mrs. Wenrich resold. He supposes Mrs. Wenrich is dead. She was a delicate old rouged widow like a doll with white hair and it always seemed funny to hear talk about greens and divots and tourneys and par come out of her mouth. Eccles parks the long Buick on the asphalt lot and says, "Before I forget."

Rabbit's hand is on the door handle. "What?"

"Do you want a job?"

"What kind?"

"A parishioner of mine, a Mrs. Horace Smith, has about eight acres of garden around her home, toward Appleboro. Her husband was an incredible rhododendron enthusiast. I shouldn't say incredible; he was a terribly dear old man."

"I don't know beans about gardening."

"Nobody does, that's what Mrs. Smith says. There are no gardeners left. For forty dollars a week, I believe her."

"A buck an hour. That's pretty poor."

"It wouldn't be forty hours. Flexible time. That's what you want, isn't it? Flexibility? So you can be free to preach to the multitudes."

Eccles really does have a mean streak. Him and Belloc. Without the collar around his throat, he kind of lets go. Rabbit gets out of the car. Eccles does the same, and his head across the top of the car looks like a head on a platter. The wide mouth moves. "Please consider it."

"I can't. I may not even stay in the county."

"Is the girl going to kick you out?"

"What girl?"

"What is her name? Leonard. Ruth Leonard."

"Well. Aren't you smart?" Who could have told him? Peggy Gring? By way of Tothero? More likely Tothero's girl Whatsername. She looked like Janice. It doesn't matter; the world's such a web anyway, things just tremble through. "I never heard of her," Rabbit says.

The head on the platter grins weirdly in the sunglare off the grease-gray metal.

They walk side by side to the cement-block clubhouse. On the way Eccles remarks, "It's the strange thing about you mystics, how often your little ecstasies wear a skirt."

"Say. I didn't have to show up today, you know."

"I know. Forgive me. I'm in a very depressed mood."

There's nothing exactly wrong with his saying this, but it rubs Harry's inner hair the wrong way. It kind of clings. It says, *Pity me. Love me.* The prickly sensation makes his lips sticky; he is unable to open them to respond. When Eccles pays his way, Harry can scarcely negotiate thanking him. When they pick out a set of clubs for him to rent, he is so indifferent and silent the freckled kid in charge stares at him as if he's a moron. The thought flits through his brain that Eccles is known as a fag and he has become the new pet. As he and Eccles walk together toward the first tee he feels dragged down, lame.

And the ball feels it too, the ball he hits after a little advice from Eccles. It sputters away to one side, crippled by a perverse topspin that makes it fall from flight as dumpily as a blob of clay.

Eccles laughs. "That's the best first drive I ever saw."

"It's not a first drive. I used to hit the ball around when I was a caddie. I should do better than that."

"You expect too much of yourself. Watch me, that'll make you feel better."

Rabbit stands back and is surprised to see Eccles, who has a certain spring in his unconscious movements, swing with a quaint fifty-year-old stiffness. As if he has a pot to keep out of the way. He punches the ball with a cramped backswing. It goes straight, though high and weak, and he seems delighted with it. He fairly prances into the fairway. Harry trails after him heavily. The soggy turf, raw and wet from recently thawing, sinks beneath his big suede shoes. They're on a seesaw; Eccles goes up, he comes down.

Down in the pagan groves and green alleys of the course Eccles is transformed. A brainless gaiety animates him. He laughs and swings and clucks and calls. Harry stops hating him, he himself is so awful. Ineptitude seems to coat him like a scabrous disease; he is grateful to Eccles for not fleeing from him. Often Eccles, fifty yards further on—he has an excited gleeful habit of running ahead—comes all the way back to find a ball Harry has lost. Somehow Rabbit can't tear his attention from where the ball *should* have gone, the little ideal napkin of clipped green pinked with a pretty flag. His eyes can't keep with where it *did* go. "Here it is," Eccles says. "Behind a root. You're having terrible luck."

"This must be a nightmare for you."

"Not at all. You're extremely promising. You never play and yet you haven't once missed the ball completely."

This does it; Harry sets himself and in the murderous strength of his desire to knock it out in spite of the root he misses the ball completely.

"Your only mistake is trying too hard," Eccles says. "You have a beautiful natural swing." Rabbit whacks again and the ball flops out and wobbles a few yards.

"Bend to the ball," Eccles says. "Imagine you're about to sit down."

"I'm about to lie down," Harry says. He feels sick, giddily sick, sucked deeper into a vortex whose upper rim is marked by the tranquil tips of the leafing trees. He seems to remember having been up there once. He skids into puddles, is swallowed by trees, infallibly sinks into the mangy scruff at the sides of the fairways.

Nightmare is the word. In waking life only animate things slither and jerk for him this way. His unreal hacking dazes his brain; half-hypnotized, it plays tricks whose strangeness dawns on him slowly. In his head he is talking to the clubs as if they're women. The irons, light and thin yet somehow treacherous in his hands, are Janice. *Come on, you dope, be calm; here we go, easy.* When the slotted clubface gouges the dirt behind the ball and the shock jolts up his arms to his shoulder, his thought is that Janice has struck him. *So dumb, really dumb. Screw her. Just screw her.* Anger turns his skin rotten, so the outside seeps through; his insides go jagged with the tiny dry forks of bitter scratching brambles, where words hang like caterpillar nests that can't be burned away. *She stubs stubs fat she stubs the dirt* torn open in a rough brown mouth *dirt stubs fat:* with the woods the "she" is Ruth. Holding a 3-wood, absorbed in its heavy reddish head and grass-stained face and white stripe prettily along the edge, he thinks *O.K. if you're so smart* and clenches and swirls. *Ahg:* when she tumbled so easily, to balk at this! The mouth of torn grass and the ball runs, hops and hops, hides in a bush. And when he walks there, the bush is damn somebody, his mother; he lifts the huffy branches like skirts, in a fury of shame but with care not to break any, and these branches bother his legs while he tries to pour his will down into the hard irreducible pellet that is not really himself yet in a way is; just the way it sits there white and Number 1 in the center of everything. As the 7-iron chops down *please Janice just once* awkwardness spiders at his elbows and the ball as he stares bending one way bends the other way into more sad scruff further on, the khaki color of Texas. *Oh you moron go home.* Home is the hole, and above, in the scheme of the unhappy vision that frets his conscious attention with an almost optical overlay of presences, the mild gray rain sky is his grandfather waiting upstairs.

And, now at the corners, now at the center of this striving golf dream, Eccles flits in his grubby shirt like a white flag of forgiveness, crying encouragement, fluttering from the green to guide him home.

The greens, still dead from the winter, are salted with a dry dirt: fertilizer? The ball slips along, making bits of grit jump. "Don't stab your putts," Eccles says. "A little easy swing, arms stiff. Distance is more important than aim on the first putt. Try again." He kicks the ball back. It took Harry about twelve to get up here on the fourth green, but this arrogant assumption that his strokes are past counting irritates him. *Come on, sweet,* he pleads as if with his wife, *there's the hole, big as a bucket. Everything will be all right.*

But no, she has to stab in a feeble, panicked way; what was she afraid of? The ball is maybe six feet short. Walking toward Eccles, he says, "You never did tell me how Janice is."

"Janice?" Eccles with an effort drags his attention up from the game. He is absolutely in love with winning; *he is eating me up,* Harry thinks. "She seemed in good spirits on Monday. She was out in the back yard with this other woman, and they were both giggling when I came. You must realize that for a little while, now that she's adjusted somewhat, she'll probably enjoy being back with her parents. It's her own version of your irresponsibility."

"Actually," Harry says gratingly, squatting to line up the putt, the way they do it on television, "she can't stand her parents any more than I can. She probably wouldn't've married me if she hadn't been in such a hurry to get away from 'em." His putt slides past on the down side and goes two or three fucking feet too far. Four feet. Fuck.

Eccles sinks his. The ball wobbles up and with a glottal rattle bobbles in. The minister looks up with the light of triumph in his eyes. "Harry," he asks, sweetly yet boldly, "why have you left her? You're obviously deeply involved with her."

"I *told* ja. There was this thing that wasn't there."

"What thing? Have you ever seen it? Are you sure it exists?"

Harry's four-foot putt dribbles short and he picks up the ball with furious fingers. "Well if you're not sure it exists don't ask me. It's right up your alley. If you don't know nobody does."

"No," Eccles cries in a strained voice. "Christianity isn't looking for a rainbow. If it were what you think it is we'd pass out opium at services. We're trying to *serve* God, not *be* God."

They pick up their bags and walk the way a wooden arrow tells them.

Eccles goes on, explanatorily, "This was all settled centuries ago, in the heresies of the early Church."

"I tell you, I know what it is."

"What is it? What *is* it? Is it hard or soft? Harry. Is it blue? Is it red? Does it have polka dots?"

It hits Rabbit depressingly that he really wants to be told. Underneath all this I-know-more-about-it-than-you heresies-of-the-early-Church business he really wants to be told about it, wants to be told that it is there, that he's not lying to all those people every Sunday. As if it's not enough to be trying to get some sense out of this crazy game you have to carry around this madman trying to swallow your soul. The hot strap of the bag gnaws at his shoulder.

"The truth is," Eccles tells him with womanish excitement, in a voice embarrassed but determined, "you're monstrously selfish. You're a coward. You don't care about right or wrong; you worship nothing except your own worst instincts."

They reach the tee, a platform of turf beside a hunchbacked fruit tree offering fists of taut ivory-colored buds. "Let me go first," Rabbit says. "Till you calm down." His heart is hushed, held in mid-beat, by anger. He doesn't care about anything except getting out of this tangle. He wants it to rain. In avoiding looking at Eccles he looks at the ball, which sits high on the tee and already seems free of the ground. Very simply he brings the clubhead around his shoulder into it. The sound has a hollowness, a singleness he hasn't heard before. His arms force his head up and his ball is hung way out, lunarly pale against the beautiful black blue of storm clouds, his grandfather's color stretched dense across the north. It recedes along a line straight as a ruler-edge. Stricken; sphere, star, speck. It hesitates, and Rabbit thinks it will die, but he's fooled, for the ball makes its hesitation the ground of a final leap:

with a kind of visible sob takes a last bite of space before vanishing in falling. "That's *it!*" he cries and, turning to Eccles with a grin of aggrandizement, repeats, "That's it."

Twenty years later, in the summer of 1979, Rabbit Is Rich *finds Rabbit a member of a country club, the Flying Eagle Tee and Raquet Club, ogling his golfing buddies' wives—especially one plump, young, bikini-clad Cindy Murkett—and waxing philosophical about the game. "I hit the ball O.K.," runs a typical self-appraisal, "but damned if I could score." He is still seeking to realize his potential, hitting shots alternately fat and thin and fighting off gloom: "By the time they finally get out onto the golf course, green seems a shade of black. Every blade of grass at his feet is an individual life that will die, that has flourished to no purpose." We briefly see him salvage a par from a sand trap in the Labor Day fourball:*

He wriggles his feet to root himself in the sand, keeping his weight back on his heels, and makes himself swing through with the wedge, pick it up and swing it *through*, blind faith, usually he picks it clean in his timidity and flies it over the green but in this instance with his fury at Ronnie and his glum indifference it all works out: the ball floats up on its cushioning spray of sand, bites, and crawls so close to the pin the three others of his foursome cackle and cheer. He sinks the putt to save his par. Still, the game seems long today, maybe it's the gin at noon or the end-of-summer doldrums, but he can't stop seeing the fairways as chutes to nowhere or feeling he should be somewhere else, that something has happened, *is* happening, that he's late, that an appointment has been made for him that he's forgotten.

On vacation with his friends on a Caribbean island, "riding in canopied carts down sere fairways laid out between brambly jungles from which there is no recovery," he struggles with golf tips and the oppressive sense of guilt and injustice that hangs above golf's vast spaces:

> He plays golf badly today; when he is tired he tends to overswing, and to flip his hands instead of letting the arms ride through. Keep the wrist-cock, don't waste it up at the top. Don't sway onto your toes, imagine your nose pressed against a pane of glass. Think railroad tracks. Follow through. These tips are small help today, it seems a long morning's slog between hungry wings of coral jungle, up to greens as bumpy as quilts, though he supposes it's a miracle of sorts to have greens at all under this sun. He hates Webb Murkett, who is sinking everything inside of twenty feet today. Why should this stringy old bullshitter hog that fantastic little cunt and take the nassau besides?

We don't see Harry play a round, however, until ten more years have delivered him, in Rabbit at Rest, *to retirement on the west coast of Florida and the golf course attached to his condo complex, Valhalla Village. He feels all of his fifty-five years; his chest suffers ominous twinges, and he wears glasses:*

AND THE LENSES are always dusty and the things he looks at all seem tired; he's seen them too many times before. A kind of drought has settled over the world, a bleaching such as overtakes old color prints, even the ones kept in a drawer.

Except, strangely, the first fairway of a golf course before his first swing. This vista is ever fresh. There, on the tee's earth platform, standing in his large white spiked Footjoys and blue sweat socks, drawing the long tapered steel wand of his Lynx Predator driver from the bag, he feels tall again, tall the way he used to on a hardwood basketball floor when after those first minutes his growing momentum and lengthening bounds and leaps reduced the court to childlike dimensions, to the size of a tennis court and then a Ping-Pong table, his legs unthinkingly eating the distances up, back and forth, and the hoop with its dainty skirtlike net dipping down to be there on the layups. So, in golf, the distances, the hundreds of yards, dissolve to a few effortless swings if you find the inner magic, the key. Always, golf for him holds out the hope of perfection, of a perfect weightlessness and consummate ease, for now and again it does happen, happens in three dimensions, shot after shot. But then he gets human and tries to force it, to make it happen to get ten extra yards, to steer it, and it goes away, grace you could call it, the feeling of collaboration, of being bigger than he really is. When you stand up on the first tee it is there, it comes back from wherever it lives during the rest of your life, endless possibility, the possibility of a flawless round, a round without a speck of bad in it, without a missed two-footer or a flying right elbow, without a pushed wood or pulled iron; the first fairway is in front of you, palm trees on the left and water on the right, flat as a picture. All you have to do is take a simple pure swing and puncture the picture in the middle with a ball that shrinks in a second to the size of a needle-prick, a tiny tunnel into the absolute. That would be *it*.

But on his practice swing his chest gives a twang of pain and this makes him think for some reason of Nelson, his son. The kid jangles in his mind. As he stands up to the ball he feels crowded but is impatient and hits it outside in, trying too hard with his right hand. The ball starts out promisingly but leaks more and more to the right and disappears too close to the edge of the long scummy pond of water.

" 'Fraid that's alligator territory," Bernie says sadly. Bernie is his partner for the round.

"Mulligan?" Harry asks.

There is a pause. Ed Silberstein asks Joe Gold, "What do you think?"

Joe tells Harry, "I didn't notice that *we* took any mulligans."

Harry says, "You cripples don't hit it far enough to get into trouble. We always give mulligans on the first drive. That's been our tradition."

Ed says, "Angstrom, how're you ever going to live up to your potential if we keep babying you with mulligans?"

Joe says, "How much potential you think a guy with a gut like that still has? I think his potential has all gone to his colon."

While they are thus ribbing him Rabbit takes another ball from his pocket and tees it up and, with a stiff half-swing, sends it safely but ingloriously down the left side of the fairway. Perhaps not quite safely: it seems to hit a hard spot and keeps bouncing toward a palm tree. "Sorry, Bernie," he says. "I'll loosen up."

"Am I worried?" Bernie asks, putting his foot to the electric-cart pedal a split-second before Harry has settled into the seat beside him. "With your brawn and my brains, we'll cream these oafs."

Bernie Drechsel, Ed Silberstein, and Joe Gold are all older than Harry, and shorter, and usually make him feel good about himself. With them, he is a big Swede, they call him Angstrom, a comical pet gentile, a big pale uncircumcised hunk of American white bread. He in turn treasures their Jewish perspective; it seems more manly than his, sadder and wiser and less shaky. Their long history has put all that suffering in its pocket and strides on. Harry asks Bernie, as the cart rolls over the tamped and glistening grass toward their balls, "Whaddeya think about all this fuss about this Deion Sanders? In the paper this morning he even has the mayor of Fort Myers making excuses for him."

Bernie shifts the cigar in his mouth an inch and says, "It's cruel, you know, to take these black kids out of nowhere and give 'em all this publicity and turn them into millionaires. No wonder they go crazy."

"The paper says the crowd kept the cops from giving him room. He had flipped out at some salesclerk who said he had stolen a pair of earrings. He even took a pop at her."

"I don't know about Sanders," Bernie says, "but a lot of it's drugs. Cocaine. The stuff is everywhere."

"You wonder what people see in it," Rabbit says.

"What they see in it," Bernie says, stopping the cart and resting his cigar on the edge of the plastic ledge for holding drinks or beer cans, "is instant happiness." He squares up to his second shot with that awful stance of his, his feet too close together, his bald head dipping down in a reverse weight-shift, and punches the ball with a 4-iron: all arms and wrists. It stays straight, though, and winds up within an easy chip in front of the elevated green. "There are two routes to happiness," he continues, back at the wheel of the cart. "Work for it, day after day, like you and I did, or take a chemical shortcut. With the world the way it is, these kids take the shortcut. The long way looks too long."

"Yeah, well, it *is* long. And then when you've gone the distance, where's the happiness?"

"Behind you," the other man admits.

"What interests me about Sanders and kids like that," Rabbit says, as Bernie speeds along down the sun-baked fairway, dodging fallen brown fronds and coconuts, "is I had a little taste of it once. Athletics. Everybody cheering, loving you. Wanting a piece."

"Sure you did. It sticks out all over. Just the way you waggle the club. 'Fraid you made the palm tree, though. You're stymied, my friend." Bernie stops the cart, a little close to the ball for Harry's comfort.

"I think I can hook it around."

"Don't try it. Chip it out. You know what Tommy Armour says: take your stroke in a situation like this, and go for the green on the next one. Don't attempt a miracle."

"Well, you're already up there for a sure bogey. Let me try to bend it on." The palm tree is one of those whose trunk looks like a giant braid. It breathes on him, with its faint rustle, its dim smell like that of a friendly attic full of dried-out old school papers and love letters. There's a lot of death in Florida, if you look. The palms grow by the lower branches dying and dropping off. The hot sun hurries the life cycles along. Harry takes his stance with his hip almost touching the jagged rough trunk, hoods the 5-iron, and imagines the curving arc of the miracle shot and Bernie's glad cry of congratulation.

But in fact the closeness of the tree and maybe of Bernie in the cart inhibits his swing and he pulls the ball with the hooded club, so it hits the top of the next palm along the fairway and drops straight down into the short rough. The rough, though, in Florida isn't like the rough up north; it's just spongy pale grass a half-inch longer than fairway. They tailor these courses for the elderly and lame. They baby you down here.

Bernie sighs. "Stubborn," he says as Harry gets back in. "You guys think the world will melt if you whistle." Harry knows that "guys" is polite for "goys." The thought that he might be wrong, that obstacles won't melt if he whistles, renews that dull internal ache of doom he felt in the airport. As he stands up to his third shot with an 8-iron, Bernie's disapproval weighs on his arms and causes him to hit a bit fat, enough to take the click out of the ball and leave it ten yards short.

"Sorry, Bernie. Chip up close and get your par." But Bernie fluffs the chip—all wrists again, and too quick— and they both get sixes, losing the hole to Ed Silberstein's routine bogey. Ed is a wiry retired accountant from Toledo, with dark upright hair and a slender thrusting jaw that makes him look as if he's about to smile all the time; he never seems to get the ball more than ten feet off the ground, but he keeps it moving toward the hole.

"You guys looked like Dukakis on that one," he crows. "Blowing it."

"Don't knock the Duke," Joe says. "He gave us honest government for a change. The Boston pols can't forgive him for it." Joe Gold owns a couple of liquor stores in some city in Massachusetts called Framingham. He is stocky and sandy and wears glasses so thick they make his eyes look like they're trying to escape from two little fishbowls, jumping from side to side. He and his wife, Beu,

Beu for Beulah, are very quiet condo neighbors next door; you wonder what they do all the time in there, that never makes any noise.

Ed says, "He wimped out when it counted. He should have stood up and said, 'Sure I'm a liberal, and damn proud of it.'"

"Yeah, how would that have played in the South and the Midwest?" Joe asks. "In California and Florida for that matter with all these old farts who all they want to hear is 'No more taxes'?"

"Lousy," Ed admits. "But he wasn't going to get their votes anyway. His only hope was to get the poor excited. Knock away that three-footer, Angstrom. I've already written down your six."

"I need the practice," Harry says, and strokes it, and watches it rim out on the left edge. Not his day. Will he ever have a day again? Fifty-five and fading. His own son can't stand to be in the same room with him. Ruth once called him Mr. Death.

"He was going for those Reagan Democrats," Joe continues explaining. "Except there aren't any Reagan Democrats, there're just cut-and-dried rednecks. Now that I'm down south here, I understand better what it's all about. It's all about blacks. One hundred thirty years after Abe Lincoln, the Republicans have got the anti-black vote and it's bigger than any Democratic Presidential candidate can cope with, barring a massive depression or a boo-boo the size of Watergate. Ollie North doesn't do it. Reagan being an airhead didn't do it. Face it: the bulk of this country is scared to death of the blacks. That's the one gut issue we've got."

After that episode with Skeeter twenty years ago Rabbit

has had mixed feelings about blacks and whenever the subject comes up he tends to hold his tongue lest he betray himself one way or another. "Bernie, what do you think?" Harry asks while they're watching the two others hit from the second tee, a 136-yard par-three over that same scummy pond. He finds Bernie the wisest of the three, the most phlegmatic and slowest to speak. He never came back totally from some open-heart surgery he had a few years ago. He moves cumbersomely, has emphysema and a bit of a humpback and the slack look of a plump man who lost weight because his doctor told him to. His color isn't good, his lower lip in profile looks loose.

"I think," he says, "Dukakis tried to talk intelligently to the American people and we aren't ready for it. Bush talked to us like we were a bunch of morons and we ate it up. Can you imagine, the Pledge of Allegiance, read my lips—can you imagine such crap in this day and age? Ailes and those others, they made him into a beer commercial—head for the mountains." Bernie sang this last phrase his voice quavery but touchingly true. Rabbit is impressed by this ability Jews seem to have, to sing and to dance, to give themselves to the moment. They sing at seder, he knows, because Bernie and Fern had them to a seder one April just before heading north. Passover. The angel of death passed over. Harry had never understood the word before. Let this cup pass from me. Bernie concludes, "To my mind there are two possibilities about Bush—he believed what he was saying, or he didn't. I don't know which is more terrifying. He's what we call a *pisher.*"

"Dukakis always looked like he was sore about something," Rabbit offers. This is as close as he can bring himself to admit that, alone in this foursome, he voted for Bush.

Bernie maybe guesses it. He says, "After eight years of Reagan I would have thought more people would have been sore than were. If you could ever get the poor to vote in this country, you'd have socialism. But people want to think rich. That's the genius of the capitalist system: either you're rich, or you want to be, or you think you ought to be."

Rabbit liked Reagan. He liked the foggy voice, the smile, the big shoulders, the way his head kept wagging during the long pauses, the way he floated above the facts, knowing there was more to government than facts, and the way he could change direction while saying he was going straight ahead, pulling out of Beirut, getting cozy with Gorby, running up the national debt. The strange thing was, except for the hopeless down-and-outers, the world became a better place under him. The Communists fell apart, except for in Nicaragua, and even there he put them on the defensive. The guy had a magic touch. He was a dream man. Harry dares say, "Under Reagan, you know, it was like anesthesia."

"Ever had an operation? A real operation."

"Not really. Tonsils when I was a kid. Appendix when I was in the Army. They took it out in case I was sent to Korea. Then I was never sent."

"I had a quadruple bypass three years ago."

"I know, Bern. I remember your telling me. But you look great now."

"When you come out of anesthesia, it hurts like hell. You can't believe you can live with such pain. To get at your heart, they split your whole rib cage open. They crack you open like a coconut. And they pull the best veins they can find out of your upper leg. So when you come out of it your groin's killing you as well as your chest."

"Wow." Harry inappropriately laughs, since while Bernie was talking to him on the cart Ed, with that pompous fussy setup he has, laying his hands on the club finger by finger like he's doing flower arrangement, and then peeking toward the hole five or six times before swinging, as if he's trying to shake loose cobwebs or a tick in his collar, looked up during the swing so the topped ball scuttered into the water, skipping three times before sinking, leaving three expanding, interlocking sets of rings on the water. Alligator food.

"Six hours I was on the table," Bernie is urging into his ear. "I woke up and I couldn't move. I couldn't even open my eyelids. They *freeze* you, so your blood flow is down to almost nothing. I was like locked into a black coffin. No. It's like I *was* the coffin. And then out of this blackness I hear this weird voice, with a thick Indian accent, the Pakistani anesthetist."

Joe Gold, with his partner's ball in the water, tries to hit it too quick, to get a ball in play, jerking the club back in two stages like he does and then roundhousing with that flat swing stocky guys tend to have. He pushes the shot off so he catches the pot bunker on the right.

Bernie is doing a high, spacy, Pakistani voice. " 'Ber-nie, Ber-nie,' this voice says, so honest to God I think maybe it's the voice of God, 'oper-ation a suc-cess!' "

Harry has heard the story before but laughs anyway. It's a good, scary story about the edge of death.

" 'Ber-nie, Ber-nie,' " Bernie repeats, "like it came out of the clouds to Abraham, to go cut Isaac's throat."

Harry asks, "Shall we keep the same order?" He feels he disgraced himself on the previous hole.

"You go first, Angstrom. I think it shakes you up too much to hit last. Go for it. Show these nudniks how it's done."

This is what Rabbit hoped to hear. He takes a 7-iron and tries to think of five things: keeping his head down, keeping his backswing from being too long, moving his hip while the club is still at the top, keeping his downswing smooth, and keeping the clubface square on the ball, at that point on the sphere where a clockface says 3:15. From the whistly magic way the ball vanishes from the center of his held-down vision he knows the hit is sweet; they all together watch the dark dot rise, hover that little ghostly extra bit that gives the distance, and then drop straight down on the green, a hair to the left but what looks pin high, the ball bouncing right with the slant of the bowl-shaped green.

"Beauty," Ed has to admit.

"How about a mulligan?" Joe asks. "We'll give you one this time."

Bernie asks, pushing himself out of the cart, "What iron was that?"

"Seven."

"Gonna hit 'em like that, my friend, you should use an eight."

"Think I'm past the hole?"

"Way past. You're on the back edge."

Some partner. There's no satisfying him. Like Marty

Tothero nearly forty years ago. Get twenty-five points a game, Marty wanted thirty-five and would talk about a missed layup. The soldier in Harry, the masochistic Christian, respects men like this. It's total uncritical love, such as women provide, that makes you soft and does you in.

"For me, I think a choked-up six," Bernie says.

But in trying to take something off the shot he takes off too much and leaves it short, over the water but on the bank, where it's hard to manage a stance. "Tough chip from there," Harry says, unable to resist a gentle needle. He still blames Bernie for parking the cart so close on that attempted deliberate hook.

Bernie accepts the needle. "Especially after that last shitty chip of mine, huh?" he says, pushing his cut-up, deflated, humpbacked old body into the cart, Harry having slid over into the driver's seat. The guy who's on the green has earned the right to drive. Harry feels momentum building, they're going to cream these oafs. He glides over the water on an arched wooden bridge with red rubber treads laid over the planks. "From where you are," Bernie tells him as they get out, "the green slopes down. Hit your putt too hard, you'll slide miles beyond."

Ed with a ball in the water is out of it. Bernie's stance on the steep bank is so awkward he whiffs the ball once, shanks it sideways on his next swing, and picks up. But sandy Joe Gold, in his element, waggles his feet to plant himself and manages a good blast shot out of the pot bunker. With Bernie's advice preying on his mind, interfering with his own instincts, Harry strokes his long approach putt tentatively and leaves it four feet short. He marks it with a Valhalla Village marker while Joe two-putts for his bogey. Joe takes his time and gives Harry too long to study his four-footer. He sees a break, then doesn't see it. In trying to avoid lipping out on the left like he did on the last hole, he loses his par putt, very makable, an inch to the right. "Son of a son of a *bitch*," he says, frustration pressing from behind his eyes so hard he thinks he might burst into tears. "On in one, and a fucking three-putt."

"It happens," Ed says, writing down the 4 with his trained accountant's primness. "Tie hole."

"Sorry, Bern," Harry says, climbing back into the cart, on the passenger side.

"I screwed you up," his partner says. "Should have kept my yap shut about the green being downhill." He unwraps another cigar and, pushing the pedal, leans back into a long day.

Not Harry's day. The Florida sun seems not so much a single ball overhead but a set of klieg lights that pursue you everywhere with an even white illumination. Even directly under palm trees and right up against the twelve-foot pine fences that separate the Village from the rest of the world, the sun finds you, reddening the tip of Rabbit's nose and baking his forearms and the back of his non-gloved hand, which is already dotted with little white bumps of keratosis. He carries a tube of number-15 sunscreen in his golf bag and is always dabbing it on but the ultraviolet gets through anyway, cooking his squamous cells into skin cancer. The three men he plays with never use anything and just get a comfortable tan, even the bald top of Bernie's head, as smooth as an ostrich egg with only a few small specks on it as he bends over his shots with that awful reverse-shift, squeezed-feet stance of his. Harry

feels Bernie's steady, mechanically repeating ineptitude—
short shots, chunked chips—a burden today, since he
can't quite carry him, and wonders why somebody who
exudes suffering wisdom the way Bernie does never learns
a thing about golf or even seems to try. To him, Harry
supposes, it's just a game, a way of killing time in the sun
at this stage of his life. Bernie endures retirement fun in
Florida the way he's endured his entire life, sucking that
same acrid wet-cigar taste out of it. He doesn't see what
Harry sees in the game—infinity, an opportunity for infinite improvement. Rabbit doesn't see it himself today.
Around the eleventh hole—a dogleg par-five that he
butchers, slicing his second shot, a 4-wood, so wildly it
winds up in a condo's side yard, between some plastic
trash cans and a concrete slab with some rusting steel
clothesline poles sunk in it (a German shepherd chained
to the clothesline barks at him, lunging toward him so the
taut wire sings, and Gold and Silberstein loafing in their
cart cackle, and Bernie chomps deeper and looks morose),
taking the out-of-bounds drop for a four while the dog
keeps barking and barking, trying to hit a 3-iron so hard
he digs six inches behind and sprays sand all over his shoes
and into the tops of his socks, pulling the next iron to the
left into a bed of parched and shedding azaleas beside the
twelfth tee, taking a drop for another stroke, skulling
the chip clear across over the green (all three playing partners keeping a ghastly silence now, shocked, mourning for
him, or is it holding in their glee?), plunking the next sand
shot against the trap lip so it dribbles back, and picking up
in disgust, and even hitting himself on the knee when
after raking he flips the sand rake to one side—after this
hole, the game and day begin to eat him into a state of de-

pression. The grass looks greasy and unreal, every other palm tree is dying from the drought and dropping stiff brown fronds, the condos line every fairway like tall stucco outhouses, and even the sky, where your eyes can usually find relief, is dirtied by jet trails that spread and wander until they are indistinguishable from God's pure clouds.

The hours pile on, noon comes and goes, the klieg lights begin to dim but the heat is turned up higher. They finish at quarter to three, Harry and Bernie twenty dollars down—both sides of a five-dollar nassau plus the eighteen and a press on the second nine that they lost. "We'll get 'em next time," Harry promises his partner, not really believing it.

"You weren't quite yourself today, my friend," Bernie admits. "You got girl-friend trouble or something?"

Throughout the thirty years and six months that the four novels cover, Ronnie Harrison, Rabbit's teammate on their high-school basketball team, bothersomely shadows him—"a presence he couldn't avoid, an aspect of himself he didn't want to face." Their old animosity acquired fresh cause during Harry's long, off-and-on-again affair with Harrison's wife, Thelma. Earlier in the summer of 1989, back in Pennsylvania, Rabbit has had percutaneous angioplasty and Thelma has died, of lupus erythematosus.

Now AUGUST, muggy and oppressive in its middle weeks, is bringing summer to a sparkling distillation, a final clarity. The fairways at the Flying Eagle, usually burnt-out and as hard as the cart paths this time of year, with all the rain they've had are still green, but for the rough of reddish-brown buckgrass, and an occasional spindly maple sapling beginning to show yellow. It's the young trees that turn first—more tender, more attuned. More fearful.

Ronnie Harrison still swings like a blacksmith: short backswing, ugly truncated follow-through, sometimes a grunt in the middle. No longer needed at the lot, needing a partner if he was going to take up golf again, Rabbit remembered Thelma's saying how they had had to resign from the club because of her medical bills. Over the phone, Ronnie had seemed surprised—Harry had surprised himself, dialing the familiar digits trained into his fingers by the dead affair—but had accepted, surprisingly. They were making peace, perhaps, over Thelma's body. Or reviving a friendship—not a friendship, an involvement—that had existed since they were little boys in knickers and hightop sneakers scampering through the pebbly alleys of Mt. Judge. When Harry thinks back through all those years, to Ronnie's pugnacious thick-lipped dull-eyed face as it loomed on the elementary-school playground, to Ronnie crowingly playing with his big pale cucumber of a prick (circumcised, and sort of flat on its upper side) in the locker room, and then to Ronnie on the rise and on the make in his bachelor years around Brewer, one of the guys it turned out who had gone with Ruth before Rabbit did, Ronnie in those years full of smart-ass talk and dirty stories, a slimy operator, and then to Ronnie married to Thelma and working for Schuylkill Mutual, a kind of a sad sack really, plugging along doggedly, delivering his pitch, talking about "your loved ones" and when you're "out of the picture," slowly be-

coming the wanly smiling bald man in the photo on
Thelma's dresser whom Harry could feel looking up his
ass, so once to Thelma's amusement he got out of bed and
put the photo flat on the bureau top, so afterwards she always turned it away before he arrived of an afternoon, and
then to Ronnie as a widower, with the face of a bleached
prune, pulled-looking wrinkles down from his eyes, an old
guy's thin skin showing pink at the cheekbones, Harry
feels that Ronnie has always been with him, a presence he
couldn't avoid, an aspect of himself he didn't want to face
but now does. That clublike cock, those slimy jokes, the
blue eyes looking up his ass, what the hell, we're all just
human, bodies with brains at one end and the rest just
plumbing.

Their first round, playing as a twosome, they have a
good enough time so that they schedule another, and then
a third. Ronnie has his old clients but he's no longer out
there generating new business among the young hus-
bands, he can take an afternoon off with a little notice.
Their games are rusty and erratic, and the match usually
comes down to the last hole or two. Will Harry's fine big
free swing deliver the ball into the fairway or into the
woods? Will Ronnie look up and skull an easy chip across
the green into the sand trap, or will he keep his head
down, his hands ahead, and get the ball close, to save a
par? The two men don't talk much, lest the bad blood between them surface; the sight of the other messing up is
so hilariously welcome as to suggest affection. They never
mention Thelma.

On the seventeenth, a long par-four with a creek about
one hundred ninety yards out, Ronnie plays up short with
a 4-iron. "That's a chickenshit way to play it," Harry tells

him, and goes with a driver. Concentrating on keeping his flying right elbow close to his body, he catches the ball sweet, clearing the creek by thirty yards. Ronnie, compensating, tries too hard on his next shot: needing to take a 3-wood, he roundhouses a big banana ball into the pine woods on the Mt. Pemaquid side of the fairway. Thus relieved of pressure, Rabbit thinks *Easy does it* on his 6-iron and clicks off a beauty that falls into the heart of the green as if straight down a drainpipe. His par leaves him one up, so he can't lose, and only has to tie to win. Expansively he says to Ronnie as they ride the cart to the eighteenth tee, "How about that Voyager Two? To my mind that's more of an achievement than putting a man on the moon. In the *Standard* yesterday I was reading where some scientist says it's like sinking a putt from New York to Los Angeles."

Ronnie grunts, sunk in a losing golfer's self-loathing.

"Clouds on Neptune," Rabbit says, "and volcanos on Triton. What do you think it means?"

One of his Jewish partners down in Florida might have come up with some angle on the facts, but up here in Dutch country Ronnie gives him a dull suspicious look. "Why would it mean anything? Your honor."

Rabbit feels rubbed the wrong way. You try to be nice to this guy and he snubs you. He is an ugly prick and always was. You offer him the outer solar system to think about and he brushes it aside. He crushes it in his coarse brain. Harry feels a fine excessiveness in that spindly machine's feeble but true transmissions across millions of miles, a grace of sorts that chimes with the excessive beauty of this crystalline late-summer day. He needs to praise. "Those three rings nobody ever saw before," he insists, "just like drawn with a pencil," echoing Bernie Drechsel's awe at the thinness of flamingo legs.

But Ronnie has moved off, over by the ball washer, pretending not to hear. He has a bum knee from an old football injury and begins to limp toward the end of a round. He takes a series of vicious practice swings, anxious to begin the hole and avenge his previous poor showing. Disappointed, distracted by thoughts of brave Voyager, Rabbit lets his right elbow float at the top of the backswing and cuts weakly across the ball, slicing it, on a curve as uncanny as if plotted by computer, into the bunker in the buckgrass to the right of the fairway. The eighteenth is a par-five that flirts with the creek coming back but should be an easy par; in his golfing prime he more than once birdied it. Yet he has to come out of the bunker sideways with a wedge and then hits his 3-iron—not his best club but he needs the distance—fat, trying too hard just like Ronnie on the last hole, and winds up in the creek, his yellow Pinnacle finally found under a patch of watercress. The drop consumes another stroke and he's so anxious to nail his 9-iron right to the pin he pulls it, so he lies five on the deep fringe to the left of the green. Ronnie has been poking along, hitting ugly low shots with his blacksmith's swing but staying out of trouble, on in four; so Rabbit's only hope is to chip in. It's a grassy lie and he fluffs it, like the worst kind of moronic golfing coward he forgets to hit down and through, and the ball moves maybe two feet, onto the froghair short of the green in six, and Ronnie has a sure two putts for a six and a crappy, crappy win. If there's one thing Harry hates, it's losing to a bogey. He picks up his Pinnacle and with a sweeping heave throws the ball into the pine woods. Something in his chest didn't like the big motion but it is bliss of sorts to see the tormenting orb disappear in a distant swish and thud. The match ends tied.

"So, no blood," Ronnie says, having rolled his twelve-footer to within a gimme.

"Good match," Harry grunts, deciding against shaking hands. The shame of his collapse clings to him. Who says the universe isn't soaked in disgrace?

As they transfer balls and tees and sweaty gloves to the pocket of their bags, Ronnie, now that it's his turn to feel expansive, volunteers, "Didja see last night on Peter Jennings, the last thing, they showed the photographs of the rings and the moon moving away and then a composite they had made of the various shots of Neptune projected onto a ball and twirled, so the whole planet was there, like a toy? Incredible," Ronnie admits, "what they can do with computer graphics."

The image faintly sickens Harry, of Voyager taking those last shots of Neptune and then sailing off into the void, forever. How can you believe how much void there is?

The golf bags in the rack here by the pro shop throw long shafts of shadow. These days are drawing in. Harry is thirsty, and looks forward to a beer on the club patio, at one of the outdoor tables, under a big green-and-white umbrella, beside the swimming pool with its cannon-balling kids and budding bimbos, while the red sun sinks behind the high horizon of Mt. Pemaquid. Before they head up for the beers, the two men look directly at each other, by mistake. On an unfortunate impulse, Rabbit asks "Do you miss her?"

Ronnie gives him an angled squint. His eyelids look sore under his white eyelashes. "Do you?"

Ambushed, Rabbit can barely pretend he does. He used Thelma, and then she was used up. "Sure," he says.

Ronnie clears his ropy throat and checks that the zipper on his bag is up and then shoulders the bag to take to his car. "Sure you do," he says. "Try to sound sincere. You never gave a fuck. No. Excuse me. A fuck is exactly what you gave."

Harry hangs between impossible alternatives—to tell him how much he enjoyed going to bed with Thelma (Ronnie's blue-eyed photo watching) or to claim that he didn't. He answers merely, "Thelma was a lovely woman."

"For me," Ronnie tells him, dropping his pugnacious manner and putting on his long widower's face, "it's like the bottom of the world has dropped out. Without Thel, I'm just going through the motions." His voice gets all froggy, disgustingly. When Harry invites him up on the patio for the beers, he says, "No, I better be getting back. Ron Junior and his newest significant other are having me over for dinner." When Harry tries to set a date for the next game, he says, "Thanks, old bunny, but you're the member here. You're the one with the rich wife. You know the Flying Eagle rules—you can't keep having the same guest. Anyway, Labor Day's coming. I better start getting back on the ball, or Schuylkill'll think I'm the one who died."

And it will not have escaped keen students of the game that the doctors who accompany Harry on the rounds of his cardiac ill-

ness have a certain physical resemblance to famous golfers—
Drs. Breit and Raymond, who perform the angioplasty in
Brewer, to Tom Kite and Raymond Floyd, and Dr. Olman, in
the hospital in Florida, to another Australian immigrant, Greg
Norman. Rabbit's Florida internist, who advises him to walk
and acquire "a healthy interest in life," is an elderly crabby
Scotsman, Dr. Morris, whose son, young Tom, waits to take
over the practice. The old Pennsylvania jock marooned in Val-
halla Village goes out among champions.

A GOOD ROUND
WITH TOM MARSHFIELD

*Marshfield, a forty-one-year-old clergyman, has been banished,
in my novel* A Month of Sundays, *to a month of therapeutic
seclusion at a desert resort maintained for the rehabilitation of
errant clergymen. His prescribed regimen is as follows: "Morn-
ings: write,* ad libitum. *Afternoons: physical exercise, preferably golf, though riding, swimming, tennis facilities do exist.
Evenings: board or card games, preferably poker." The directress of the place, the tall, dark-haired, impressive Ms. Prynne,
seems to read his journal entries, and in gradual displacement
of the numerous parish romances that have troubled his min-
istry he gradually falls in love with her, his ideal reader. His fellow patients are all clergymen, and those he plays golf with are:
Woody, a muscular priest rebelliously loyal to the Latin mass;
Jamie Ray, a Tennessee preacher guilty of pederasty; and Amos,
a pastor caught in the act of arson, as described herein. This is
the twenty-third chapter of the novel, that is, Marshfield's journal entry on the twenty-third day of his month of Sundays.*

· · ·

DID NOT SLEEP WELL last night. Homeward thoughts within me burning already? The first week, I slept hardly at all, it seemed; I laid down my head inside a lonely plastic droning that was proceeding west at 550 miles per hour, at a cruising altitude of 34,000 feet. Then, grain by grain, this place stopped moving, it became a *place*, and now the danger is it has become the *only* place. And this accounting the only accounting, and you my reader my only love.

Let me tell you a few golf stories. In the first week of my stay, when the contours of the course had not been sprinkled brightly into my brain (I have been thinking a lot about love, these days, my hatred of the word, and it occurs to me, one of insomnia's perishable revelations, that before we love something we must make a kind of replica of it, a memory-body of glimpses and moments, which then replaces its external, rather drab existence with a constellatory internalization, phosphorescent and highly portable and in the end impervious to reality's crude strip-mining), I played alone, the front nine, as my companions went in to their rooms, their pills, their re-morses, and their naps, and on the seventh, as the im-mense bandshell of desert sky was resonating with muted lilac on one side of the orchestra and on the other side a pink pizzicato of cloud-stipple was tiptoeing toward the cymbal-clash of a fiery sunset (hang on, it's my therapy, not yours), I came down off the hill with a solid but pushed drive and, from an awkward lie, a 5-iron that, in the way of the unexpectedly well-hit shot, went pure over the flagstick and skipped off the green. You remember, of course, how the apron on this side is a little shoulder, glazed on top by a spiked hardpan that invites a scuffed shot every time. But a power greater than myself with my own hands took a 7-iron from the bag, pictured the chip crisply, swung crisply, and watched the ball hop from the clubhead; it jiggled over some worm castings (the greens committee flies the worms in from Brazil at great expense), hit the pin with a heavenly *thunk*, and dropped in. A birdie three. Joy unweighted my long-laden heart. The next hole, of course, is that very short par-three, a mere 120 yards by the card; I took an 8-iron and a relaxed little swing, picturing the ball a-glint by the flagstick. Instead I saw it flutter sideways into the impenetrable shoulder of sage and creosote bush on the right. And *the next shot went the same way*. A brand-new Titleist. I scored myself an X on the hole and dragged back to the clubhouse. My face felt scorched; I had encountered the devil. I had brushed up against a terrible truth: it's the sure shots that do us in.

Or, to put the moral in a more useful form, even a half-hit demands a shoulder-turn.

And a full intention: lukewarm I spit thee out.

Golf is as it were all bones, an instant chastener and teacher; lessons glow through, shapely as the graphs of binomial equations, that would hide forever amid the muffling muscle of lived life's muddle.

Here a more human story, and happier for your hero. Last week we were in our usual foursome—me, Jamie Ray, Amos, and Woody. Woody and I had on our usual dollar nassau, and as usual he was outdriving me by fifteen yards. I don't see how he ever got those shoulders into a cassock, and don't wonder the Vatican decided he needed a cooling off. Every time he thinks about the de-Latinized

Mass his face goes red as a lobster and his claws begin to rattle. He got Jamie Ray as partner today, which meant he was sure to collect on the team play. Jamie Ray swings miserably but putts like an angel; I sometimes wonder if buggery hasn't made the hole look relatively huge to him. Whereas we poor cunt men keep sliding off to the side, hunched over as fearful as fetuses who suddenly realize they can never push their craniums through a three-and-a-half-inch pelvic opening. Amos must have been a rapist once, for he tries to hit the back of the cup so hard a miss (and most are) runs two or three yards past. I know, of course, dear directress, that Amos's crisis was asexual. We've all spilled our beans, though forbidden to. He was the pastor of a happy little outer-inner-city church, wooden colonial, all pillar and pew, annual budget around thirty thou, two hundred families on the rolls, maybe fifty active. A cheerfully dying little situation, no strain on a man of sixty, head bald as an onion, arthritis creeping into the joints, children off in Teheran and Caracas working for the government or the oil companies, an arthritic evangelical faith kept a little limber by the sprinkling of blacks in the flock and a lot of civic busywork in the "community at large." Suddenly, the church burns down. Faulty wiring? Panther-Muslim vandals from the ghetto one neighborhood away? A loose Jovebolt? No matter, in a great rally of solidarity and if-God-be-on-our-sidism they voted to rebuild, and did, a spiffyish little altar-in-the-round job of cream-colored pressed-garbage bricks, shaped like a hatbox with a hatpin pointing out and upwards. The only trouble was, no one came. The blacks thought the money should have gone into community action, the old faithfuls couldn't stand the new architecture, the younger element took to tripping in one another's basements and calling it devotions, and the rich family that had principally contributed never came anyway, having lived here when this outer-inner city was working pasture at the end of the trolley tracks and still believing that the religious duties of a squirearchy were fully absolved by a Christmastide appearance. Amos's wife and Korean foster-child attended services, and some of the local teenagers who thought they were possessed would break in nights and do things on the altar that left damp spots, and the volleyball and yoga groups thrived upstairs; but it wasn't enough for Amos. The emptiness, the silence, the mortgage payments, the shoddy workmanship and materials of the new building, the funny smell when it rained—they got to him. His custodian found him one Saturday night in the furnace room soaking newspapers in kerosene, and here he is among us.

But you know that story, and I began to tell another. Golf. Golf, gold, good, gods, nods, *nous*, gnus, anus, Amos. Eight strokes, with some cheating and a one-putt. Amos's golf had the peculiarity that, no matter with what club he struck the ball, from driver to wedge, the arc was the same—low and skulled-looking. But he was straight, and could be depended upon for a customary bogey, leaving me free (free! a word to be put into the stocks along with *love:* one an anarchist, the other a fornicator) to go for the pars. Still, against a hot putter and a big hitter, what hope was there? Precious little. A saving remnant. Woody had me three holes up with four to go. On the fifteenth he hooked his drive into the pond. "*Unum baptisma in remissionem peccatorum,*" I said to him, and drove short with an iron for a safe five. Three left and two down. A

comfortable cushion, his shoulders implied, my little ban-
derilla of Latin quivering as yet unfelt. Or perhaps felt
as an unneeded surge of divine afflatus, for he overswung
his fairway wood on the spacious sixteenth fairway and
topped it badly; it scuttered into a prairie-dog burrow. At
least, it vanished, in that band of scruff bordering the ar-
royo. The four of us circled for ten minutes, like old
women gathering fuel in vacant lots you might say, before
giving up. *"Qui tollis peccata mundi,"* I consoled my priestly
opponent, and complacently (I confess it) chipped my
own, indifferent but safe shot onto the green, for another
winning bogey. Jamie Ray had run into trouble in a
bunker, and Amos found the dead center of the back of
the cup, so we saved some quarters on the team debt as
well. Woody felt the world sliding; as we teed up for the
par-three seventeenth, I beheld descend upon him for the
first time the possibility that his lead might dissolve entirely. He was rattled; he was excited; the Latin had
tripped open sluices of *excessus* in him. He surprised me
unpleasantly by popping a 6-iron onto the dead center of
the green, which slopes toward the sunset, California, and
the Sea of Peace that bulges up at the infinite like an un-
blinkered eyeball. My own 5-iron took a lucky kick and
appeared against the glare to creep onto the right edge of
the green. Neither were Amos nor Jamie Ray in trouble.
Hosannah.

One must walk down steps of orange shale here. The
light was so nice, our evening drinks were so close, our
match was so amusing—slung among us loosely like a
happy infant in a blanket we each held a corner of—that
we talked loudly in our joy, and once on the green I, the
first to putt, lifted my arms and incanted, *"Pleni sunt coeli*

et terra gloria tua." You may or may not be surprised to know, my ms.terious Ms., that they have licensed me as the clown of the group.

Nothing clownish, however, I pictured the line of my long putt so firmly it became a Platonic Ideal in my mind, as hyperreal as a cubic inch of Sirius would be on Earth, in the second before its weight collapsed the examining table and burned a tidy square tunnel straight to China; and I stroked the lag, and, while it did not go into the cup, it trailed in close enough for a gimme, which is pretty fair from fifty feet. Woody, ruddy with the sunset glow and the remembrance of the Mass spoken as God meant it to be, not unpredictably powered his fifteen-footer half as many feet past on the downhill side, and in sudden consternation putted short coming back, and took a squandered four to my struggled three. One to go, and all even. Our friends were amazed. I was a miracle-worker even if like many another miracle-worker I came to a sad end.

And of course I did not. Pure, floating, purged of all dross, my swing drove the ball a sobbing seventh of a mile toward the edge of the sun; Woody, pressing but not destroyed, was one swale shorter, but straight. He hit (Amos and Jamie Ray poking along beside us like men pushing peanuts with their nose) first, and a cloud momentarily muted my sense of transcendence as I saw that his shot was a beautiful thing, hitting behind the pin so hot it backed up. Yet, out of love for you, Ms. Prynne, among others, I took a 7-iron and gazed from the height of my compact and unhurried backswing at the ball on its crystalline plane of sparkling sand and grass until more suddenly than a melted snowflake it vanished. My divot leaped, which they don't usually do.

I let my head lift. Oh, with what a sublime comet's curve was that shot bending gently in, from the half-set sun's edge to the tilted flagstick. I lost the ball in the shimmer of the green, but my glad bones guessed it was inside his. And so it was. Our walking revealed the balls in a line with the cup, his ten feet past, mine five feet short. And still the priestly devil, the minion of the Babylonian mother of harlots, gave battle. His putt, stroked with a Jesuitical fineness, broke away at the last minisecond, as his ally the snivelling Dixie pederast grunted. Whereas my problematical five-footer, too confidently stroked from within my trance of certain grace, would have slid by on the high side had not a benign warp of the divine transparence deflected it; it teetered around half the hole's circumference, but the eventual glottal rattle there could be no denying. My partner, stout Amos, applauded. My opponent looked at me webbily, through the crazed windshield of his shattered faith. *"O salutaris hostia,"* I saluted him, and felt myself irradiated by the Lordly joy of having defeated—nay, crushed, obliterated—a foe.

Tomorrow we would all be resurrected, and play again.

THE GOLF-COURSE PROPRIETOR

(One of a Series of "Interviews with Insufficiently Famous Americans")

HE SITS by the little clubhouse, in a golf cart, wearing black. He is Greek. Where, after all these years in America, does he buy such black clothes? His hat is black. His shirt is black. His eyes, though a bit rheumy with age now, are black, as are his shoes and their laces. Small black points exist in his face, like scattered punctuation. His smile is wonderful, an enfolding of the world as his hand enfolds yours. Many little gray teeth, all his, they must be: something of the ancient marriage of tragedy and comedy in that smile.

How ancient is he? He has been sitting here since one learned golf twenty years ago. In those years, it was his son who manned the tractor with his gang of mowers, going up and down the fairways as methodically as a lover's caresses. Now it is his grandson. Once, in Homeric times, it must have been he, Theodoros, who manned the tractors. But times so epic are hard to imagine.

The first, second, third, and ninth holes can be seen from where he sits, and the fourth tee, where many a man has been tempted by the broad downhill leftward dogleg to hook into the marsh. The ridge holds its writhing occupants in profile, a frieze against the sky, before they mourn their shots, pocket their tees, and drag their carts down into the underworld. The fifth, sixth, seventh, and eighth holes are entirely out of sight, but the men in their bright slacks eventually return, advancing down the ninth fairway like a thinned army pulling its own chariots. Their odyssey ends in a ritual exchange with the owner, who has that essential capacity mythic characters have for waiting, waiting decades if need be, for the foreordained moment in the adventure to arrive.

Q: How goes it, Teddy, how goes it?
A: Not so good, John, not so good.
Q: Lovely day out there.
A: [*nods*]

Weather and health are discussed but never, oddly, golf. What does he know about golf? Among the mysteries that radiate as he in his black clothes soaks up the sun are:

Q: How did he come to acquire this frivolously utilized acreage?
Q: Does it turn a profit?
Q: What *is* this Greek genius for acquisition?

The questions go unanswered. The seasons turn from spring (raw winds, patchy greens, plugged drives) to summer (insect repellent, lost balls) to fall (morning dew, goose feathers, baked fairways, terrific roll); the tractor mows back and forth, back and forth, on the contours of the course. Teddy is aging. He is shrinking in the golf cart, his handclasp grows feverish, his eyes misty; he disappears. Over the winter, one hears he has had a stroke. Speculation is rife. The course will be sold, a thousand ranch houses will spring up.

In the spring, the golfers return, in cleated rubbers, but he is not here. The golf cart sits empty, like Agamemnon's throne. The dandelions come, the greenhead flies, the August thunderstorms. Suddenly, he is there. His black clothes are faded to gray, and his face matches his clothes. He searches one's face almost blindly, through his feeble enfolding of the offered hand.

Q: How goes it, Teddy, how goes it?

A: Τις δ' οἰδεν εἰ το ζην μεν ἐστι κατϑανειν, το κατϑανειν δε ζην κατω νομιζεται.*

Q: We thought you were dead. What's your secret?

A: [*gestures toward golf course*]**

---

*Translation: Who knows if life is death, and death is considered life in the world below? [Euripides]

**Translation: He will not die. He is land, and land does not die.

GOLF AS A GAME OF THE PEOPLE

No OTHER GAME (lest it be polo) is as thoroughly associated with capitalism and its oppression as golf. Years ago, I played the six holes of the only remaining course in Romania under the eye of an antique pro who had caddied for King Michael; otherwise, in the Communist world scarcely a tee or green exists, and China's recently announced decision to build some courses in effect announces her secession from that world.* The Hollywood movies of the Depression era showed the rich swaggering from the eighteenth green straight into their tuxedos, and to this day golf, in the magazines devoted to it and in the televised tournaments, puts forward an image of luxury, of lush grass and palatial clubhouses, of bronzed, trim, gray-haired men swapping swing tips and stock tips in a dappled atmosphere of having it all. The very length of time the game consumes implies lives rich in leisure, and its

---

*How things have changed, globally, in the ten years since I wrote this piece! *What* Communist world?

space implies folks able to afford a playground the size of three farms.

And yet in the United States hundreds of humble golf layouts exist where workingmen, children, retirees, and housewives of modest social pretension lose themselves in the bliss and aggravation of the sport. At ten minutes after four, in many a provincial setting, the first tee is thronged as the factory league shows up, to play in rolled-up shirt-sleeves, and the competition continues until deepest dusk swallows the ball. Next morning, early, the elderly arrive, their foursomes as fixed and repetitive as their cautious swings, for the invariable daily round. Then, in mid-morning, the brigade of the fair sex, having given the housework a lick, appears; brown-legged, broad-beamed, they pull pastel-colored carts, wear visors and bobby socks, and concede no putts on the green. In the summer, children, variously sized and shaped but predominantly male, go around and around the course, swinging a mis-matched assortment of rusty clubs, lackadaisically poking at the shrubbery and shuffling through the rough in the hope of finding lost balls. The daily mob, costumed in tank tops and cut-offs, sneakers and baseball hats, leaves the rough downtrodden and turns grass tees into dust bowls; but what a harvest of pleasure springs from acres so democratically exploited! I learned the game—or, rather, began to learn that I would never quite learn it—on such overused, undermaintained public courses, and can report that they yield delights unknown to those who have al-ways stepped on the spongy turf of private fairways. These delights include:

Teeing off on rubber mats. The white ball really stands out against the black rubber, and, for those who tend to hit behind the ball, the clubhead gets a good sharp bounce where sod would smother it. Hitting the ball on the bounce imparts a lot of topspin, which, on a parched and threadbare fairway, adds unbelievable yardage to a scuffed drive.

Lots of broken tees lying around, to hit irons off of on the par-threes. One of the disadvantages of an expensive private club is that the crew cleans these up every day, and you have to take a perfectly good tee and break it yourself.

No trouble with lies near sprinkler heads, since there are no sprinkler heads.

Nice bushy greens, since without a watering system the grass has to be left long or will turn the color and crunchy texture of toast. So a good firm putting stroke can be indulged without fear of more than a gimme if you run past. Also, the abundance of worm castings, unrepaired ball marks, rabbit and groundhog spoor, and the like injects a relaxing element of chance into the putting and induces a carefree, humorous attitude you will never see on the impeccable fast surfaces of, say, Augusta National.

Sand bunkers whose initial load of sand has long since been stolen away by erosion. The ball can be played with a choked-up mid-iron, as if from a swale in the fairway.

Volunteer anthill bunkers. Especially well-developed on courses south of the Mason-Dixon Line, anthills qualify as ground under repair. Ants do not qualify, however, as greenskeepers, and can be brushed from the line of the putt.

Winter rules all summer long. You can always improve your lie on a rough-hewn public course, and amid the hardpan there are lots of little tummocks to nudge the ball up onto.

Castrated rough. To keep play moving on your average overpopulated public course, the rough has been cut back until only the most sweeping slice or electrifying hook can find any growth grabbier than a welcome mat.

Dodgem. The land at the disposal of the designer (if any) was, in many cases, exiguous, so the fairways are narrow and closely intertwined. I have even known fairways to cross, like railroad tracks, or to merge over the horizon, like parallel lines in non-Euclidean geometry. Other players' golf balls are frequent arrivals in the middle of practice swings, or during shot contemplation. That whistle just by your ear wasn't a quail flying home, and that thudding at your back doesn't mean a hailstorm. The other-ball hazard gives an invigorating edge to a sport many consider tame, and also produces the pleasant social phenomenon of

Inter-foursome communication, or voices across the fairways. "I beg your pardon, did you just hit my ball?" "What kind was it?" "A yellow Pinnacle." "A yellow Pinnacle what?" "I forget. Maybe a three." "*Mine* was a three, too. Did the one you hit have a little pink smudge on it, from where I shanked it off the ball washer?" "I don't know. I didn't look." "You ought to look." "For pink smudges? Be reasonable. Hey, buddy, over there—isn't that your yellow Pinnacle?" "Where?" "*There.* You blind?" "You're the one who's blind—that's a dandelion." "Heads up!" "*Ouch!*" "Too bad. Some people, huh? They ought to at least have yelled 'Fore!' What make is it, anyway?" "A Hogan two. With some insurance-company logo on it." "Why don't you go ahead and hit it, quick? The guy's looking the other way, and he probably gets them for free." "O.K., it's a deal. [*Hits.*] Have a nice day." "You, too, my friend."

With such exchanges and interlacing of shots, a camaraderie builds up that extends the breadth and width of the course, as if on some huge volleyball court.

Nor does the bonhomie end when the last hole is played. A hearty thirst and sense of righteous struggle reward the player at every level. No deleterious alcoholic beverages, however, are brought by uniformed manservants onto the clubhouse veranda for the players of the people's game. Instead, there is a cozy shack, with old balls redeemed from the pond in a jar marked *3 for $2*, Milky Ways growing stale in a dusty case, a little tree of potato-chip bags, and a veteran fridge stocked with Coke, Dr Pepper, and—for a real taste from the past—chocolate milk. Perhaps, too, there is a screened-in porch, where the exhausted players can sit and chortle over the card, pay off their quarter bets, and watch others three-putt the bumpy ninth green. You change your shoes in the car, and take a shower when you get home. The membership costs nothing, but the sense of belonging is just as keen as at Winged Foot or Baltusrol. You belong to golf, and you elected yourself.

THE BIG BAD BOOM

GOLF IS GOING GREAT, the front page of *The New York Times* announced last fall. "Golf is the fastest-growing sport in America," it quoted the director of publicity for the National Golf Foundation in Jupiter, Florida, as saying. Nearly half a billion rounds of golf, nearly a billion dollars spent on balls, bags, clubs, and carts. Everything is up, up, from tour prize money to subscriptions to *Golf Galore*. Women, blacks, and yuppies are all discovering in golf, we read, "a serene setting, low impact exercise and a matchless opportunity for networking." Nearer home to me, the Boston *Globe* confirms the golf boom. One out of nine Massachusetts residents are golfers, combining for eleven million rounds last year and spending approximately $371,000,000 on the game, over seventeen million for balls alone. Ten times that was spent on greens fees, with forty-eight million going for golf carts. Hooray for golf, I guess.

The truth is, I wish it were half as popular, the way it was when I took up the game thirty-odd years ago. For in those decades, in the area where I live, north of Boston, the number of public golf courses has increased not at all, and courses that used to be a breeze to play have become simply hellish. You wait on the tee, in a mob of impatient foursomes, for an hour or more. Finally launched, you wait on every shot except the putts for the group ahead to clear, and on some short holes the bunch-up at the tee is three foursomes deep. The old courtesies implode in the crush. Nobody thinks to wave the next group on or to repair a ball mark on the green. Youthful couch potatoes, testing the outdoors in tank tops, Hawaiian surfing shorts, and waffle-sole running shoes, scoot around in their carts whacking divots out of the helpless turf and never thinking to replace one. The grassed tees are as pitted and dusty as Sahel cattle runs. The management has given up replacing the stolen and broken sand-trap rakes. The greens have the texture of cork dart boards under high magnification. The course isn't just overplayed, it's pillaged.

The owners of these courses shouldn't be blamed; they should be thanked for not selling off the acreage to a developer and retiring to West Palm Beach with their millions. The population pressure on Northeastern golf courses is fierce. When a new one does get built, after years of wrangling with local planning boards and distant creditors, the course is intensely private and so laden with condominiums between the fairways that playing it is like taking a walk in a housing development. No: it *is* taking a walk in a housing development. Men sprinkling their lawns, women slamming the doors of their station wagons as they unload groceries—you feel like a ridiculous trespasser. You feel like that old *Punch* cartoon showing a gent in plus-fours toting his baffie in the desert, his sweating caddie tagging behind, asking an Arab on camelback, "Is this the way to the water hazard?"

Meanwhile, back on the public courses, mayhem reigns. To speed the play of the stampeding herds, trees are cut down, out-of-bounds stakes multiply, sand bunkers are grassed in, cart paths rim the fairways with asphalt, carts become obligatory. The charm of walk-along, rough-and-ready golf will soon be just a memory, like sand-lot baseball and the old swimming hole. When I, a free-lance writer with an odd afternoon to spare, began to play golf, a comfortable array of nearby public courses stood ready to indulge me. First, there was the little layout in my own town of Ipswich, nine holes squeezed into a low-lying corner field. The vistas were nil and the odds were high of getting hit by somebody else's golf ball. Yet you could take your eight-year-old son to play there, or your eighty-year-old grandmother, and not feel embarrassed. The pace was slow but the course was short, and an adolescent boy with nothing better to do could go around six times a day, as my son and his pals used to. In its very exiguity the layout taught the virtues of a straight ball and, from off the tiny greens, a deft chip.

Next step up on the local ladder was a more spacious nine-hole course two miles down the road, in the clam-digging, shipbuilding town of Essex. The fourth tee spectacularly overlooked miles of salt marsh and oceanic inlets, the seventh green was on a natural island, and only two of the par-fours could be called Mickey Mouse. At that stage of my golf evolution, however, no hole was Mickey Mouse to me, and the days I broke a hundred there, and then ninety, and then—in one mad confluence of easy swings and lucky putts—eighty, remain in my mind as happy, happy days. My foursome used to meet at two in the afternoon, play around twice, have a beer and bag of ripple chips in an adjacent tavern, and be home by six o'clock.

Twenty minutes in another direction, toward New-buryport, another nine-hole course challenged us with el-evated greens and two par-fives that ended just short of the horizon. In Topsfield, a relatively new course called New Meadows offered a testing succession of pine-lined fairways permeated by the traffic hum of Route One. In yet another nearby town, Wenham, an eighteen-hole course had been worked into some hilly terrain, flattering one's scorecard with an opening gust of par-threes but moving into a back nine of some grandeur, along the rail-road tracks that carried our less holiday-minded acquain-tances back from a hard day in Boston. For golfers willing to venture a half-hour in from the coast, there were the romantically designated Far Corner in West Boxford, Hickory Hill on the edge of Dracut, and Colonial in Wakefield, where an occasional Red Sox player could be spotted on leave from Fenway Park.

And so on. There were lots of courses, the point is, and if you were professionally situated to avoid the weekends all of them were a pleasure to play, for single-digit greens fees at that. Now, when I and those of my playing com-panions who have survived the onslaught of years venture back to one of these remembered paradises, we are as Adam and Eve expelled—the halcyon vistas are crowded with traffic, the turf is littered with non-biodegradable trash, and even the snakes have been trampled to death.

I was spoiled, you could say. While I was blithely spraying shots in the backwoods of New England, the golfers of Queens were sleeping in their cars to get a morning tee-time and the resourceful Japanese were building multitiered driving-ranges in Tokyo. Golf, born on the sandy waste links of Scotland, is engaged, like farms, wildlife, and old-fashioned burial grounds, in a losing battle for the precious planetary surface. Economics dictates that new golf courses can only be built as carpeting between condos, or as private retreats for the scarily rich. For those who can't make a big investment, there's always bowling. You can do bowling at night, and you never lose a ball.

I was lucky enough to have been allowed to join, before the boom became quite so thunderous, a private club. It had been a relaxed sort of place—a shaggy old layout where Willie Anderson had won a couple of U.S. Opens when the century was still in kneepants. You could walk the eighteen without seeing more than two or three houses peeking in at the edges, and scarcely more than that number of other golfing groups. The same man who cut the lawn in front of the veranda was the head greenskeeper. The sun and the chinch bugs were pretty much allowed to have their way with the verdure, and the underground pipes installed in the days of Bobby Jones had become pure ferric oxide, but, on balance, who terribly cared? On a balmy summer day, there was still nothing in the world to come between you and par except your own ineptitude. Golf's gift to the spirit is space, and the space in this case was organically designed and blessedly, blissfully underpopulated.

Alas, progress has found us out. Beefy young stockbrokers with metal woods multiply on the practice range.

Snickering members of other clubs, visiting for the odd member-guest tournament, put us on the defensive about our burnt-out ninth green (I always thought it made it easier to hit, all that brown) and the wilderness of volunteer oaks and poison ivy beneath the elevated tee on the twelfth. A dynamite young technician, with all the appropriate advanced agronomical degrees, has been hired to revive the course, and so he has, to the tune of a new sprinkling system involving more trenchwork than the First World War. Dues, as irresistibly as tree sap, rise each spring. Improvements abound: an indoor practice range, with net and Astroturf; a winter program, for the new Eskimo members; and enough golf clinics and therapy groups to keep six assistant pros busy. The old course is a treasure, and the secret is out. Many a summer noon, one shows up in tattered chinos and muddy Footjoys only to be turned away by a battalion of madras-slacked, Gucci-shod executives who have seized the course for the corporate outing of some data-processing encampment along Route 128. As colorful as jungle parrots, our corporate guests rev up their carts and coat the emerald fairways with shining tire tracks.

Everything is better, golf is booming, and yet something has gone from the game—the sweet sensation of being alone, in the tawny buffalo-grass rough, with a problem to be solved at your own pace. If, like the composer of this lament, you regard golf as a physical as well as a social exercise and still like to walk a course, carrying your bag on your shoulder, it is a loss to be made to feel guilty by the networking young bucks in their electric chariots, pressing you impatiently from behind. Something kindred happened when clay and grass tennis courts were replaced by HarTrue, and when you could no longer stand up straight in your ski boots.

High tech can't replace nature's gifts. Golf used to be a kind of breather, and it has become more and more hard-breathing. Compare the tone of present tournament broadcasts with those of the Fifties, when television golf was mostly a matter of the charming *Shell's Wonderful World of Golf,* a series of staged matches dominated by the relaxed personalities and swings of Sam Snead and Jimmy Demaret. Now the talk into the microphone mostly concerns how many tens of thousands this or that putt is worth. Even the dollars are bunching up in line.

Will success spoil golf? For public-course players, I could say it already has. For private-course players, it's made the sport more mechanical and mirthless. Big-bucks golf-glamour, get lost. Try skeet-shooting for a change. The clay-pigeon commercials alone should be worth billions.

THE CAMARADERIE OF GOLF—I

ONE EVENING LAST SUMMER, a golfing companion of mine, his wife, my wife, and I set out toward an art movie whose line, when we showed up, proved to be too long and too young. Youths of indeterminate sex, with heads like paint-bespattered thistles, scowled at us in their sullen multitudes, and with the wisdom of our gray hairs we turned and fled. Since we had already bolted down hamburgers, and babysitters blocked a graceful return to our homes, this left us with some hours to kill. Cruising a dismal semi-industrial zone foisted upon a stretch of cattailed swamp, we came upon a brightly lit and totally unattended miniature-golf course, its little lighthouses and paddle wheels waiting with forlorn cheer in the sulphurous glow of bug-zappers nibbling away at the night's infinite supply of insects; in a giddy burst of revived adolescence, my pal and I persuaded our spouses to stop and play eighteen quick holes with us.

These ladies, in their teetery platform clogs and soigné art-movie frocks, made an awkward spectacle at first on the rubber tees, concrete fairways, and outdoor-carpet greens of the little course, but when both of them sank long putts (my wife on the testing, windmill-guarded short second; her counterpart answering right back on the tricky dogleg third, banking it through a big tin funnel and off of a plywood cutout of Bullwinkle the Moose) they began to get into the spirit of the sport, and the smokestacks and cattails echoed with our hilarity, our good-natured joshing, our rising competitive frenzy. I, just as in the big game, had difficulties keeping the ball in play, several times hopping it over the three-inch edge boards onto the clamshell paths and once losing it entirely in the mazy entrails of a construction called Santa's Castle. My pal, true to *his* form, kept driving long but putting short. "No guts!" I would gleefully shout, or else murmur sagely, "You had the line, but not the distance."

Unaccountably, at about the eleventh hole, our wives began to show signs of ennui, and to talk about bug bites and—we had solicitously supervised their stances at the outset—backaches. After coming off of a heartbreaking seven-putt on an especially deceptive green, my wife headed for the car and locked herself in. The other wife played a few more holes, but polo-style, swinging the club left-handed as she sashayed along. Her black silk skirt was slit up to mid-thigh, and several dump trucks, making night deliveries to a nearby landfill project, tooted as they passed, which may have thrown off her stroke.

Still, our party had proven, up through the eleventh hole at least, that there is nothing intrinsically homosexual about golf camaraderie. A playing companion of any sex, religion, or place of national origin becomes a dear friend, caught up with us in this captivating travail. However little compatible they appear off the course, we love our fellow golfers as we tilt, sway, and crumble toward the nineteenth hole. My first experience of this camaraderie occurred, indeed, with an aging aunt, who kept praising my unbridled power while she chipped and putted me to death.

Mutual praise, or appreciation, or, at the lowest ebb, simple mute witness constitutes the essence of golf fellowship. Solitary golf is barren fun, unless we fantasize the helpful remarks of phantom companions. "Great swing," one comrade will pronounce with unction, after you whiff. "Well, at least you can find it," another will console you, after a horrendous foozle skitters to a stop on the cart path. "It was a tough lie," the third will lugubriously commiserate, as a skulled 5-iron finds eternal repose in the scum-coated heart of the lagoon. My regular foursome faithfully votes upon, at the end of the round, "the Most Ignominious Shot"—the bunker blast that bounced backward, for instance, or the twelve-inch putt that lipped out—and the shot, recollected in beery tranquillity, develops a charm that at the time passed quite unnoticed. The joys of retrospect, indeed, are so much a part of golf camaraderie that one sometimes seems to be playing the game in the future-perfect tense, with a ring of reminiscence even as the ball is struck. Golf is a game of the mind and soul as much as of the muscles and, without companionship, as pointless as a one-man philosophical symposium.

A player does best, of course, by playing the course, concentrating on each shot as if upon an aesthetic enterprise far removed from competition's grapple. Inwardly gloating upon an opponent's slice into the forest often produces, a minute later, the identical slice on one's own part. Golfing woes have a contagious quality; many the time I have seen the same easy par-four, butchered in un- canny unison, be won by a shame-faced six. Knowing that a chip and two putts will win a hole, how often do we fluff the chip and leave it entangled in the short rough, or else charge the long putt and miss the five-foot return? No, golf is not like the sweaty bash and counter-bash of tennis or the remorseless mental grind of chess. We *share* a golf match, which is part hike, part contest, part demonstra- tion, and part lesson. The good will induced by the per- ilous joint venture leads to a mutual solicitude; advice and praise are offered to an opponent as freely as to a partner. The trend of golfing rules and custom, since the hard- nosed old days of caddie-flogging and the stymie, is to- ward elaborate niceness; we repress our coughs while others are swinging, we join in the hopeless hunt for an- other's lost ball, and on the green we avoid stepping in one another's putting lines in a veritable Morris dance of exaggerated courtesy. Our behavior, ideally, is better here than elsewhere, because we are happier here than elsewhere. Golf camaraderie, like that of astronauts and Antarctic explorers, is based on a common experience of transcendence; fat or thin, scratch or duffer, we have been somewhere together where non-golfers never go.

THE CAMARADERIE OF GOLF—II

MANY MEN are more faithful to their golf partners than to their wives, and have stuck with them longer. The loyalty we feel toward our chronic consorts in golf acquires naturally the mystical and eternal overtones that the wedding ceremony hopefully, and often vainly, invokes. What is the secret? Structure, I would answer: the golf foursome is constructed with clear and limited purposes denied the nebulously grand and insatiable goals of the marriage twosome.

Like the golf course itself, golf camaraderie is an artifice, carved from the vastness of nature; it asks only five or six hours a week, from the jocular greetings in the noontime parking lot and the parallel donning of cleats in the locker room to the shouted farewells in the dusk, as the flagsticks cast their long shadows. Within this finity, irritations, jealousies, and even spats do occur, but they are mercifully dulled and dampened by the necessary distances of the game, the traditional reticence and mannerliness of sportsmen, and the thought that it will all be soon over. As in marriage, there is sharing: we search for one another's lost balls, we comment helpfully upon one another's defective swings, we march more or less in the same direction, and we come together, like couples at breakfast and dinner, on the tees and on the greens. But, unlike marriage, golf is war from the start: it is out of its regulated contention, its mathematical bloodshed, that the fervor of golf camaraderie blossoms and, from week to week, flourishes. We slay or are slain, eat or are eaten: golf camaraderie is founded on the solid and ancient ground of animal enmity, pleasantly disguised in checked slacks and small courtesies.

In many sports, such as tennis, one player's superiority over another is quickly established and monotonously reaffirmed. The inexhaustible competitive charm of golf, for the non-professional player, lies in its handicap strokes, whereby all players are theoretically equalized and an underdog can become, with a small shift of fortunes, a top dog. The drama of this shift, or the relative collapse of a stronger player, is appreciated by all, even those victimized by it. "Drama" is a key word, for golf is, within the arena of the foursome, not only war but theatre; each player has a golf persona, a predictable character, which the hazards of play subject to unpredictable shifts of fate by turns hilarious, thrilling, heroic, and pathetic. We are actors and audience in swift alternation; our love of one another is the love that enthralled spectators bear toward performers, heightened by the circumstance that the spotlight visits everyone, as the honor falls.

Much of the pleasure of golf, then, resides in the familiarity of the partners, and one's own security within a type-cast role. For years, strange to say, I played in a foursome in which I was considered the best. Not innately the best, perhaps; but another man, whose swing was sounder and who would have made short work of me in his prime, had become elderly, and had seen his scores succumb to ever-shorter drives and fits of senile chipping. In my role as tiny golfing giant, I felt tall, swung easy, and expected the putts to drop. And they often did, confidence and feeling comfortable being a significant part of golfing success. In the same era, as someone's guest on a strange course, a quick audition might establish me as the worst of the foursome, and I would play the part to perfection, straining too far back on every backswing, hurrying into every downswing, and feebly chuckling as the ball bobbled and sliced into every available rough, trap, and thicket. My only comfort, and a bleak one it was, lay in the consciousness of playing my part; I might be only Caliban, but I was saying my lines. On one such occasion, I recall, I inadvertently, combining the wrong club choice with a mis-hit, landed the ball on the green of a long par-three, and then helplessly fulfilled the unspoken expectation of my grimlipped partner: I three-putted and once again failed to help our team. In my own comfortable foursome, I would have with contemptuous ease rolled the approach putt up for a tap-in par.

When I think of that dear old foursome, two of whose members are now dead, I think of my partner's choppy impatiently baseball swing, his right foot, for all of our urging to the contrary, inflexibly bolted to the earth, and of our other opponent's irrepressible tendency to look up

and gronkle.* There is a comedy to consistency of character which we salute with laughter, as a kind of mechanical
marvel (try to gronkle on purpose; it can hardly be done)
and proof of the world's basic orderliness. And yet, when
our friend the gronkler forgot to lift his head and so sent
a shot singing into the air, this won the laughter that
greets a surprise. Good or bad, there is joy on the golf
course, and a curious sense of intimacy bred from repeated observation of this one strange physical act, the
striking of a small ball with a long L-shaped stick. Without delving into politics, love-lives, or religious views, one
seems to know golf companions very well.

In the quartet of comedians and agonists in which I
now customarily play, I am type-cast as the third-best, or
second-worst. It is a pleasant spot, suitable to my retiring
nature; one can now and then ascend to second-best sta-
tus without assuming any of the real responsibilities of
excellence, and a descent into the worst has the com-
pensation of immensely cheering up the fourth-ranked.
We are dominated, the worst and I, by a fortyish former
collegiate golf champ who, under a regimen of Buddhist
meditation and no-starch diet, has become longer and
longer off the tee—grotesquely long, in fact, so that even
his half-wedge approaches tend to float over the green
into areas rarely visited—and by an older, cannier man
whose snatchy backswing and patchy vision are less of a

---

*This term may be less universal than I realize. In our local circles, it
means, roughly, a topped ball, but a ball topped in such a way that it
comes to a halt, behind some inconvenient undergrowth, about thirty
yards distant from point of imperfect contact. It's as if the ball were
struck with the edge of the end of a broad, somewhat warped board.

handicap than they should be. He in his effervescence provides a running commentary on his shots, and heightens our sense of being on camera, for some cosmic Viewer who sits in an easy chair behind the clouds, the passing birds, the swaying treetops. We are, my beloved comrades and I, that afternoon's entertainment; our camaraderie has the subtle frenzy of show business, the makeup and glitter of it, as our fortunes ebb and flow and we live up to our roles or momentarily step out of them. The good feelings that golf breeds are inseparable from its aura of being out in the open—of being enacted within a wide and breezy transparency that leaves no shortcoming hidden and no happy stroke uncongratulated.

FARRELL'S CADDIE

WHEN FARRELL SIGNED UP, with seven other aging members of his local Long Island club, for a week of golf at the Royal Caledonian Links in Scotland, he didn't foresee the relationship with the caddies. Hunched little men in billed tweed caps and rubberized rain suits, they huddled in the misty gloom as the morning foursomes got organized, and reclustered after lunch, muttering as unintelligibly as sparrows, for the day's second eighteen.

Farrell would never have walked thirty-six holes a day in America, but here in Scotland golf was not an accessory to life, drawing upon one's marginal energy; it *was* life, played out of the center of one's being. At first, stepping forth on legs one of which had been broken in a college football game forty years before, and which damp weather or a night of twisted sleep still provoked to a reminiscent twinge, he missed the silky glide and swerve of the accustomed electric cart, its magic-carpet suspension above the whispering fairway; he missed the rattle of spare balls in the retaining shelf, and the round plastic holes to hold drinks, alcoholic or carbonated, and the friendly presence on the seat beside him of another gray-haired sportsman, another warty pickle blanching in the brine of time, exuding forbearance and the expectation of forbearance, and resigned, like Farrell, to a golfing mediocrity that would make its way down the sloping dogleg of decrepitude to the level green of death.

Here, however, on the heather-rimmed fairways, cut as close as putting surfaces back home, yet with no trace of mower tracks, and cheerfully marred by the scratchings and burrows of the nocturnal rabbits that lived and bred beneath the impenetrably thorny, waist-high gorse, energy came up through the turf, as if Farrell's cleats were making contact with primal spirits beneath the soil, and he felt he could walk forever. The rolling treeless terrain, the proximity of the wind-whipped sea, the rain that came and went with the suddenness of thought—they composed the ancient matrix of the game, and the darkly muttering caddies were also part of this matrix.

That first morning in the drizzly shuffle around the golf bags, his bag was hoisted up by a hunched shadow who, as they walked together in pursuit of Farrell's first drive (good contact, but pulled to the left, toward some shaggy mounds), muttered half to himself, with those hiccups or glottal stops the Scots accent inserts, "Sandy's wha' th' call me."

Farrell hesitated, then confessed, "I'm Gus." His given name, Augustus, had always embarrassed him, but its shortened version seemed a little short on dignity, and at the office, as he had ascended in rank, his colleagues had settled on his initials, "A. J."

"Ye want now tae geh oover th' second boosh fra' th'

laift," Sandy said, handing Farrell a 7-iron. The green was out of sight behind the shaggy mounds, which were covered with a long tan grass that whitened in waves as gusts beat in from the sea.

"What's the distance?" Farrell was accustomed to yardage markers—yellow stakes, or sprinkler heads.

The caddie looked reflectively at a sand bunker not far off, and then at the winking red signal light on the train tracks beyond, and finally at a large bird, a gull or a crow, winging against the wind beneath the low, tattered, blue-black clouds. "Ah hunnert thirhty-eight tae th' edge o' th' green, near a hunnert fifty tae th' pin, where they hu' 't."

"I can't hit a seven-iron a hundred fifty. I can't hit it even one forty, against this wind."

Yet the caddie's fist, in a fingerless wool glove, did not withdraw the offered club. "Siven's what ye need."

As Farrell bent his face to the ball, the wet wind cut across his eyes and made him cry. His tears turned one ball into two; he supposed the brighter one was real. He concentrated on taking the clubhead away slowly and low to the turf, initiating his downswing with a twitch of the left hip, and suppressing his tendency to dip the right shoulder. The shot seemed sweet, soaring with a gentle draw precisely over the second bush. He looked toward the caddie, expecting congratulations or at least some small sign of shared pleasure. But the man, whose creased face was weathered the strangely even brown of a white actor playing Othello, followed the flight of the ball as he had that of the crow, reflectively. "Yer right hand's a wee bit froward," he observed, and the ball, they saw as they climbed to the green, was indeed pulled to the left, into a deep pot bunker. Furthermore, it was fifteen yards short.

The caddie had underclubbed him, but showed no sign of remorse as he handed Farrell the sand wedge. In Sandy's dyed-looking face, pallid gray eyes showed like touches of morning light; it shocked Farrell to suspect that the other man, weathered though he was, and bent beneath the weight of a perpetual golf bag, was younger than himself—a prematurely wizened Pict, a concentrate of Farrell's diluted, Yankeefied Celtic blood.

The side of the bunker toward the hole was as tall as Farrell and sheer, built up of bricks of sod in a way he had never seen before, not even at Shinnecock Hills. Rattled, irritated at having been unrepentantly underclubbed, Farrell swung five times into the damp, brown sand, darker and denser than any sand on Long Island; each time, the ball thudded short of the trap's lip and dribbled back at his feet. " 'it at it well beheend," the caddie advised, "and dinna stop th' cloob." Farrell's sixth swing brought the ball bobbling up onto the green, within six feet of the hole.

His fellow Americans lavished ironical praise on the tardily excellent shot but the caddie, with the same deadpan solemnity with which Farrell had repeatedly struck the ball, handed him his putter. "Ae ball tae th' laift," he advised, and Farrell was so interested in this quaint concept—the ball as a unit of measure—that his putt stopped short. "Ye forgot tae 'it it, Goos," Sandy told him.

Farrell tersely nodded. The caddie made him feel obliged to keep up a show of golfing virtues. Asked for his score, he said loudly, in a stagey voice, "That was an honest ten."

"We'll call it a six," said the player keeping score, in the forgiving, corrupting American way.

As the round progressed, through a rapid alternation of brisk showers and silvery sunshine, with rainbows springing up around them and tiny white daisies gleaming underfoot, Farrell and his caddie began to grow into one another, as a foot in damp weather grows into a shoe. Sandy consistently handed Farrell one club too short to make the green, but Farrell came to accept the failure as his own; his caddie was handing the club to the stronger golfer latent in Farrell, and it was Farrell's job to let this superior performer out, to release him from his stiff, soft, more than middle-aged body. On the twelfth hole, called "Dunrobin"—a seemingly endless par-five with a broad stretch of fairway, bleak and vaguely restless like the surface of the moon, receding over a distant edge marked by two small pot bunkers, with a pale-green arm of gorse extending from the rabbit-undermined thickets on the left—his drive clicked. Something about the ghostly emptiness of this terrain, the featurelessness of it, had removed Farrell's physical inhibitions; he felt the steel shaft of the driver bend in a subtle curve at his back, and a corresponding springiness awaken in his knees, and he knew, as his weight elastically moved from the right foot to the left, that he would bring the clubface squarely into the ball, and indeed did, so that the ball—the last of his Titleists, the others having already been swallowed by gorse and heather and cliffside scree—was melting deep into the drizzle straight ahead almost before he looked up, with his head still held sideways as if pillowed on his right ear, just like the pros on television. He cocked an eye at Sandy. "O.K.?" asked Farrell, mock-modest but also genuinely fearful of some hazard, some trick of the layout, that he had missed taking into account.

"Gowf shot, sirr," the caddie said, and his face, as if touched by a magic wand, crumpled into a smile full of crooked gray teeth, his constantly relit cigarette adhering to one corner. Small matter that Farrell, striving for a repetition of his elastic sensations, topped the following 3-wood, hit a 5-iron fat and short, and skulled his wedge shot clear across the elevated green. He had for a second awakened the golf giant sleeping among his muscles, and imagined himself now cutting a more significant figure in the other man's not quite colorless, not quite indifferent eyes.

Dinner, for this week of foreign excursion, was a repeating male event, involving the same eight Long Island males, their hair growing curly and their faces ruddy away from the arid Manhattan canyons and air-conditioned offices where they had accumulated their small fortunes. They discussed their caddies as men, extremely unbuttoned, might discuss their mistresses. What does a caddie want? "Come on, Freddie, *'it* it fer once!" the very distinguished banker Frederic M. Panoply boasted that his had cried out to him as, on the third day of displaying his cautious, successful, down-the-middle game, he painstakingly addressed his ball.

Another man's caddie, when asked what he thought of Mrs. Thatcher, had responded with a twinkle, "She'd be a good 'ump."

Farrell, prim and reserved by nature, though not devoid of passion, had relatively little to offer concerning Sandy. He worried that the man's incessant smoking would kill him. He wondered if the tips he gave him were too far below what a Japanese golfer would have bestowed. He feared that Sandy was becoming tired of him. As the week went by, their relationship had become more intuitive. "A six-iron?" Farrell would now say, and without word would be handed the club. Once he had dared decline an offered 6, asked for the 5, and sailed his unusually well-struck shot into the sedge beyond the green. On the greens, where he at first had been bothered by the caddie's explicit directives, so that he forgot to stroke the ball firmly, Farrell had come to depend upon Sandy's advice, and would expertly cock his ear close to the caddie's mouth, and try to envision the curve of the ball into the center of the hole from "an inch an' a fhingernail tae th' laift." He began to sink putts. He began to get pars, as the whitecaps flashed on one side of the links and on the other the wine-red electric commuter trains swiftly glided up to Glasgow and back. This was happiness, bracketed between sea and rail, and freedom, of a wild and windy sort. On the morning of his last day, having sliced his first drive into the edge of the rough, between a thistle and what appeared to be a child's weathered tombstone, Farrell bent his ear close to the caddie's mouth for advice, and heard, "Ye'd be better leavin' 'er."

"Beg pardon?" Farrell said, as he had all week, when the glottal, hiccupping accent had become opaque. Today the acoustics were especially bad; a near-gale off the sea made his rain pants rattle like machine guns and deformed his eyeballs with air pressure as he tried to squint down. When he could stop seeing double, his lie looked fair— semi-embedded. The name on the tombstone was worn away. Perhaps it was merely an ancient railroad right-of-way marker.

"Yer missus," Sandy clarified, passing over the 8-iron.

"Ere it's tae late, mon. She was never yer type. Tae proper."

"Shouldn't this be a wedge?" Farrell asked uncertainly.

"Nay, it's sittin' up guid enough," the caddie said, pressing his foot into the heather behind the ball so it rose up like ooze out of mud. "Ye kin reach with th' eight," he said. "Go fer yer par, mon. Yer fauts er a' in yer mind; ye tend t' play a hair defainsive."

Farrell would have dismissed Sandy's previous remarks, as a verbal mirage amid the clicks and skips of wind-blown Scots, had they not seemed so uncannily true. "Too proper" was exactly what his college friends had said of Sylvia, but he had imagined that her physical beauty had been the significant thing, and her propriety a pose she would outgrow, whereas thirty-five married years had revealed the propriety as enduring and the beauty as transient. As to leaving her, this thought would never have entered his head until recently; the mergers-and-acquisitions branch had recently taken on a certain Irma Finegold, who had heavy-lidded eyes, full lips painted vermilion, and a curious presumptuous way of teasing Farrell in the eddies of chitchat before and after conferences, or in the elevator up to the boardroom. She had been recently divorced, and when she talked to Farrell she manipulated her lower lip with a pencil eraser and shimmied her shoulders beneath their pads. On nights when the office worked late—he liked occasionally to demonstrate that, well-along though he was, he could still pull an all-nighter with the young bucks—there had been between him and Irma shared Chinese meals in greasy take-out cartons, and a joint limo home in the dawn light, through the twinned arches and aspiring tracery of the

Brooklyn Bridge. And on one undreamed-of occasion, there had been an invitation, which he did not refuse, to delay his return to Long Island with an interlude at her apartment in Park Slope. Though no young buck, he had not done badly, it seemed to him, even factoring in the flattery quotient from a subordinate.

The 8-iron pinched the ball clean, and the Atlantic gale brought the soaring shot left-to-right toward the pin. "Laift edge, but dinna gi' th' hole away," Sandy advised of the putt, and Farrell sank it, for the first birdie of his week of golf.

Now, suddenly, out of the silvery torn sky, sleet and sunshine poured simultaneously. While the two men walked at the same tilt to the next tee, Sandy's voice came out of the wind, "An' steer clear o' th' MiniCorp deal. They've laiveraged th' company tae daith."

Farrell studied Sandy's face. Rain and sleet bounced off the brown skin as if from a waxy preservative coating. Metallic gleams showed as the man studied, through narrowed eyelids, the watery horizon. Farrell pretended he hadn't heard. On the tee he was handed a 3-wood, with the advice, "Ye want tae stay short o' th' wee burn. Th' wind's come around beheend, bringin' th' sun with it."

As the round wore on, the sun did struggle through, and a thick rainbow planted itself over the profile of the drab town beyond the tracks, with its black steeples and distillery chimneys. By the afternoon's eighteen, there was actually blue sky, and the pockets of lengthening shadow showed the old course to be everywhere curvaceous, crest and swale, like the body of a woman. Forty feet off the green on the fourteenth ("Whinny Brae"), Farrell docilely accepted the caddie's offer of a putter, and rolled it up and over the close-mown irregularities within a gimme of the hole. His old self would have skulled or fluffed a chip. "Great advice," he said, and in his flush of triumph challenged the caddie: "But Irma *loves* the MiniCorp deal."

"Aye, 't keeps th' twa o' ye taegither. She's fairful ye'll wander off, i' th' halls o' corporate power."

"But what does she see in me?"

"Lookin' fer a father, th' case may be. Thet first husband o' hers was meikle immature, an' also far from yer own income bracket."

Farrell felt his heart sink at the deflating shrewdness of the analysis. His mind elsewhere, absented by bittersweet sorrow, he hit one pure shot after another. Looking to the caddie for praise, however, he met the same impassive, dour, young-old visage, opaque beneath the billed tweed cap. Tomorrow, he would be caddying for someone else, and Farrell would be belted into a business-class seat within a 747. On the home stretch of holes—one after the other strung out beside the railroad right-of-way, as the Victorian brick clubhouse, with its turrets and neo-Gothic windows, enlarged in size—Farrell begged for the last scraps of advice. "The five-wood, or the three-iron? The three keeps it down out of the wind, but I feel more confident with the wood, the way you've got me swinging."

"Th' five'll be ower an' gone; ye're a' poomped up. Take th' four-iron. Smooth it on, laddie. Aim fer th' little broch."

"Broch?"

"Wee stone fortress, frae th' days we had our own braw king." He added, "An' ye might be thinkin' aboot takin' early retirement. Th' severance deals won't be so sweet aye, with th' coomin' resaission. Ye kin free yerself up, an' take on some consults, fer th' spare change."

"Just what I was thinking, if Irma's a will-o'-the-wisp."

"Will-o'-the-wisp, d' ye say? Ye're a speedy lairner, Goos."

Farrell felt flattered and wind-scoured, here in this surging universe of green and gray. "You really think so, Sandy?"

"I *ken* sae. Ye kin tell a' aboot a man, frae th' way he gowfs."

UPON WINNING ONE'S FLIGHT
IN THE SENIOR FOUR-BALL

Oh, where have they gone to—the 8-iron stiff to the
    pin,
after two less fortunate shots, setting up a par;
the calmly stroked putt that snatched a win away
from the staggered opponents; the heroic long drive
that cleared the brook on the fly by a foot or two;
the bravely slashed wedge that lifted the plugged ball
up in a sea-spray of sand to bobble gamely toward the
    hole?

How can these feats matter so little, so soon after
they mattered so much? The blood thrumming in the
    temples,
the rushes of love for one's doughty, erratic partner,
the murderous concentration upon imaginary
abstractions carved in the air by sheer sinew and
    bone—
boiled down to a trinket of silver, a tame patter
of applause in the tent, a pleasantry, a kind of loss.

GOLFERS

One-gloved beasts in cleats, they come clattering
down to the locker room in bogus triumph, bulls
with the *pics* of their pars still upright in them,
breathing false fire of stride, strike, stride, and putt.
We dread them, their brown arms and rasp of money,
their slacks the color of ice cream, their shoes,
whiter than bones, that stipple the downtrodden green
and take an open stance on the backs of the poor.

Breathing of bourbon, crowing, they strip:
the hair of their chests is grizzled, their genitals
hang dead as practice balls, their blue legs twist;
where, now, are their pars and their furor?
Emerging from the shower shrunken, they are men,
mere men, old boys, lost, the last hole a horror.

Loving the Game

THE BLISS OF GOLF

I NEVER TOUCHED A CLUB until I was twenty-five. Then, on a shady lawn in Wellesley, a kind of aunt-in-law showed me how to hold her driver and told me, after one swoop at a phantom ball, that I had a wonderful natural swing. Since that fatal encouragement, in many weathers inner and outer, amid many a green and winding landscape, I have asked myself what the peculiar bliss of this demanding game is, a bliss that at times threatens to relegate all the rest of life, including those sexual concerns that Freud claims are paramount and those even more basic needs that Marx insists must be met, to the shadows.

The immensities of space, beside which even polo and baseball are constricted pastimes, must be part of it. To see one's ball gallop two hundred and more yards down the fairway, or see it fly from the face of an 8-iron clear across an entire copse of maples in full autumnal flare, is to join one's soul with the vastness that, contemplated from another angle, intimidates the spirit, and makes one feel small. As it moves through the adventures of a golf match, the human body, like Alice's in Wonderland, experiences an intoxicating relativity—huge in relation to the ball, tiny in relation to the course, exactly matched to that of the other players. From this relativity is struck a silent music that rings to the treetops and runs through a Wagnerian array of changes as each hole evokes its set of shots, dwindling down to the final putt. The clubs in their nice gradations suggest organ pipes.

There is a bliss to the equipment—the festive polyester slacks, the menacing and elevating cleated shoes, the dainty little gauntlet the left hand gets to wear, the leathery adhesion of the grips and the riflelike purity of the shafts, the impeccable lustre of the (pre–Day-Glo orange) ball. The uniform sits light, unlike the monstrous armor of the skier or the football player, and cloaks us in a colorful individuality—not for the golfer the humiliating uniforms, cooked up by press agents and tyrannic owners, inflicted upon baseball players. We feel, dressed for golf, knightly, charging toward distant pennants past dragon-shaped hazards. The green when it receives us is soft, fine, gently undulating, maidenly.

A beautiful simplicity distinguishes the game's objective and the scoring. One stroke, count one. William Faulkner's *The Sound and the Fury* opens with an idiot watching a game of golf, and he grasps the essence well enough: "They took the flag out, and they were hitting. Then they put the flag back and they went to the table, and he hit and the other hit." That's how it goes; golf appeals to the idiot in us, and the child. What child does not grasp the pleasure-principle of miniature golf? Just how childlike golf players become is proven by their frequent inability to count past five. There is a lovable injustice, a comic democracy, in the equality, for purposes of scoring, of a three-hundred-yard smash from an elevated tee and a three-inch tap-in. Or, let's not forget, a total whiff—the most comical stroke of all. A ground-out in baseball or a tennis ball whapped into the net is not especially amusing; but bad shots in golf are endless fun—at least the other fellow's are. The duck hook, the banana slice, the topped dribble, the no-explode explosion shot, the arboreal rico-chet, the sky ball, the majestic OB, the pondside scuff-and-splash, the deep-grass squirt, the cart-path shank, the skull, the fat hit, the thin hit, the stubbed putt—what a wealth of mirth is to be had in an afternoon's witnessing of such varied miseries, all produced in a twinkling of an eye by the infallible laws of physics!

And the bliss of the swing. The one that feels effortless and produces a shot of miraculous straightness and soar. "I'll take it," we say modestly, searching about with a de-mure blush for the spun-away tee. Just a few shots a round keep us coming back; what other sport offers such sudden splendor in exchange for so few calories of expended en-ergy? In those instants of whizz, ascent, hover, and fall, an ideal self seems mirrored. If we have that one shot in us, we must have thousands more—the problem is to get them out, to *let* them out. To concentrate, to take one's time, to move the weight across, to keep the elbow in, to save the wrist-cock for the hitting area, to keep one's head still, down, and as full of serenity as a Zen monk's: an am-bitious program, but a basically spiritual one, which does not require the muscularity and shapeliness of youth. What other sport holds out hope of improvement to a man or a woman over fifty? True, the pros begin to falter at around forty, but it is their putting nerves that go, not their swings. For a duffer like the abovesigned, the room for improvement is so vast that three lifetimes could be spent roaming the fairways carving away at it, convinced that perfection lies just over the next rise. And that hope, perhaps, is the kindest bliss of all that golf bestows upon its devotees.

IS THERE LIFE AFTER GOLF?

LIKE A RELIGION, a game seeks to codify and lighten life. Played earnestly enough (spectatorship being merely a degenerate form of playing), a game can gather to itself awesome dimensions of subtlety and transcendental significance. Consult George Steiner's hymn to the fathomless wonder of chess, or Roger Angell's startlingly intense meditations upon the time-stopping, mathematical beauty of baseball. Some sports, surely, are more religious than others; ice hockey, fervent though its devotees be, retains a dross of brutal messiness, and handball, though undoubtedly it has its fine points, has not generated many holy books. Golf, on the other hand, inspires as much verbiage as astrology. In the television era, the sport has added to its antiquity and air of privilege the cachet of sudden fame and fortune earned by broad-backed boys from Latrobe, Pennsylvania, and El Paso, Texas. Millions now trudge out to the dawn starting lines inwardly clutching a tip from the Saturday sports page or the driving-range pro; an esoteric cult has become a mass cult while remaining esoteric. In Palmer's disastrous lapses, in Casper's persistent slump, golf reasserts its essential enigma. It is of games the most mysterious, the least earthbound, the one wherein the wall between us and the supernatural is rubbed thinnest. The exaltation of its great spaces; the eerie effortlessness of a good shot; the hellish effortfulness of a bad round; the grotesque disparity between a drive that eats up two-thirds of the fairway and the ten-yard dribble hit with an almost identical swing; the unpredictable warps and turns of fortune in the game; its tranced silences; its altering perspectives; its psychosomatic sensitivity to our interior monologue and the sway of our moods; the sullen, menacing sheen the monotonous grass can suddenly assume; the quirks of visibility; the dread of lostness; the ritual interment and resurrection of the ball at each green—such are the ingredients that make golf seem a magic mirror, an outward projection of an inner self. Even the most mechanical-minded books about golf evoke, for initiates, the game's verdant mysteries; Michael Murphy, in his curious and benign memoir *Golf in the Kingdom*, takes these mysteries as his major topic.

Mr. Murphy, a Californian, is a co-founder of the Esalen Institute, described on the book jacket's back flap as "a research and development center established to explore those trends in the behavioral sciences, religion, and philosophy which emphasize the potentialities and values of human existence." On the back of the jacket he is grinning with perfect teeth, and but for a faraway, faintly metaphysical gleam in his eyes he might be one of the interchangeable square-jawed young pros who clutter the tournament circuit with their competence. His book appears to be as open as his visage—he talks about himself as harried executive and student truth-seeker; he names friends and gives dates, he describes rounds of golf we do not doubt he has played. Yet the basic autobiographical episode, involving a Scots guru/pro named Shivas Irons, is, like the name itself, frankly fantastic. The book liltingly begins:

> In Scotland, between the Firth of Forth and the Firth of Tay, lies the Kingdom of Fife—known to certain lovers of that land simply as "The Kingdom." There, on the shore of the North Sea, lies a golfing links that shimmers in my memory—an innocent stretch of heather and grassy dunes that cradled the unlikely events which grew into this book. . . . There I met Shivas Irons, introduced to me simply as a golf professional, by accident one day in June 1956. I played a round of golf with him then, joined him in a gathering of friends that evening, followed him into a ravine at midnight looking for his mysterious teacher, watched him go into ecstatic trance as the sun came up, and left for London the following afternoon—just twenty-four hours after we had met—shaken, exalted, my perception of things permanently altered.

Mr. Murphy was on his way to India, to study philosophy and practice meditation with the seer Aurobindo, and it may be that he retrospectively assigned much of what he learned there to this mythical golf instructor, who plays supernaturally well, keeps a library of the occult in his digs, and, in the dead of the night, scores a hole-in-one with a feather-stuffed ball and an antique shillelagh belonging to an immortal hermit named Seamus MacDuff. Yet the course, called Burningbush, is by its location and layout recognizably St. Andrews—golf's holy place. The book never totally strays from its base subject of golf, and it even contains some practical tips: Don't strain after a good score, play it as it lies, don't seek total control. "Let the nothingness into yer shots," Shivas tells Murphy—a memorable admonition to all of us who, not trusting the unconscious mechanics of the swing, smother the ball with too much hand and arm action. When Murphy tenses up on the first tee, Shivas makes a gesture that eases him "into a feeling of stomach and hips, making a center there for my swing." The well-worn advice "Hit from the inside" is metaphysicalized to "Ken the world from the inside." Warming to his theme of "true gravity," Shivas bids his pupil "feel yer inner body." Murphy, evidently a natural athlete, travels, club in hand, through a number of yogalike states (he feels like an hourglass, then enormously tall), and sees turquoise "auras" expand and contract, and experiences other vivid intimations of "energy-dimensions" that might more disturb than settle your average twenty-handicapper. Unity and harmony are the goals of Shivas' instruction; imagine the ball and the "sweet spot" on the club as one, he says. Further, see and feel "the club and ball as one unbroken field." Further still, "sometimes a path appears in your mind's eye for the ball to follow: let it blend with your body." Murphy recalls a moment on Burningbush when all his senses joined: "For the moment . . . the world was a single field of music, joy, and light." Shivas has the ultimate word: "Aye ane fiedle [always one field] afore ye e're swung."

This religious bias, which would break down the opposition between game and player, between striker and thing struck, between man and landscape, comes as alien to the Occidental followers of aggressive Yahweh and tragic Jesus. This Occidental, for one, remains suspicious of a cosmic philosophy that so easily devolves into golf instruction. Murphy, drawing upon Shivas' supposed journals, has little trouble expanding the first part of his book, the golf part, into the comprehensive mysteries of the second. Because of the lightness of the golf ball (one and a half ounces), Shivas is led to conclude that the world, too, is feather-light, "an earthy nothingness." It is also "an icon of Man the Multiple Amphibian, a smaller, waffled version of the crystal ball, a mirror for the inner body; it is a lodestone, an old stone to polarize your psyche with." Its whiteness suggests (hello, Melville) the terror of the hueless void; its flight serves as "reminder of our hunting history and our future powers of astral flight." The hole is another mystery, linked to nostrils and other significant bodily apertures; Jean-Paul Sartre is called in to testify (from *Being and Nothingness*): "A good part of our life is passed in plugging up holes, in filling empty places, in realizing and symbolically establishing a plenitude." Not all such symbol-spinning is vapid, but it does border on the facile and the fanciful—less mysticism than mystchief. And it reduces, in practice, all this talk about luminous bodies and manifesting planes, about *hamartia* and *darshan*, about Agni the Primal Fire and the Net of Jewels, to something like witchcraft. The victory of Jack Fleck over Ben Hogan in the 1955 Open, for instance, is explained to have been Fleck's appropriation of Hogan's "inner body," and Murphy relates that while watching a baseball game he and his neighbors in the stands set up a "psychic firestorm" that permanently injured the opposing pitcher's arm. Even if it works, is black magic what we need now? " 'Tis a thin line," Shivas himself says, " 'tween the madness of God and the madness of the Devil."

The Western spirit longs for a peaceable creed that would flatter the flesh instead of mortifying it, that would blur away the painful mind-body split and ease the agonies of egoism. But these wisdoms imported from the Orient have a disturbing way of melting into physical therapy—of a harmless, deep-breathing, sweet-swinging sort—and trivial spookiness. In regard to traditional Christian problems like the existence of evil and the paradoxes of ethical action, *Golf in the Kingdom* says little. During the raucous symposium that follows his round of golf with Shivas, Murphy claims, there was a "lively discussion of shanking and the problem of evil," but we never hear it. Murphy/Shivas does offer, for the length of a page, ethical distinctions between "Mind-at-Large" and "Higher Self"; it is good to know the latter before you drown in the former. LSD is distinguished from disciplined contemplation, moral entropy from nirvana. "Ye need a solid place to swing from," Shivas says, which is half of the truth; you also need a spot to aim at. Shivas would be a complete prophet if the world were a golf course and life a game. In a game, purposes and means are indisputably ordained; in golf, rules regulate the most minute points of etiquette and equipment. A golf wherein some players were using tennis rackets and hockey pucks, some were teeing off backward from the green to the tee, and some thought the object of the game was to spear other players with the flagsticks—such a contest might produce a philosophy we could carry everywhere. As it is, analogies should be very tenderly extended outward from an island that, like golf, has been created as an artificial haven from real problems. Even within the analogy, Murphy is limited by his natural happiness at the game; for a description of the infernal misery possible *within* golf, read George Plimpton's *The Bogey Man*, especially the terrifying chapter wherein Plimpton practices with four golf balls on a tinselly, night-lit par-three course in the desert, each ball diabolically possessed of individual bad habits.

Yet there is much wit and good will in *Golf in the Kingdom*. "We are spread wide as we play, then brought to a tiny place" beautifully describes both golf and life. And why *not* make the world more of a golf course, where our acts would take validity from within, and we would replace our divots in apology for each blow, and joy would attach to the leisurely walking, the in-between times? There is a goodness in the experience of golf that may well be, as Mr. Murphy would have it, a *pitha*, "a place where something breaks into our workaday world and bothers us forevermore with the hints it gives."

Golf in the Kingdom put me in mind of another curious devotional work, William Price Fox's *Doctor Golf*, published in 1963 and long out of print. Doctor Golf, a fanatic even quainter and keener than Shivas Irons, runs a thirty-nine-member golf sanctuary in Arkansas called Eagle-Ho, refers to "young Hagen," advocates caddie-flogging, sells by mail order a clanking, cumbersome line of golf paraphernalia, and conducts a large correspondence. When one correspondent writes, "I am in my 65th year and I have been seized by golf like a mouse in the claws of a golden eagle," Doctor Golf congratulates him:

> Only after the fetters of youth have been flung aside can golf enter. Only then can the man know the folly of his adolescent belief of the swing answering to the man and

perceive the joy and the truth of the complete man answering to the swing.

And, as the years and the eagles cascade by, the even greater joy is realized when he stands in the bright sunlight of complete fulfillment and comes to realize that the *swing is the man*.

The swing is the man. The Dance of Shiva, Michael Murphy concludes, is at the heart of everything. Doctor Golf is more mystical still:

The swing by its very nature transcends the human form. The swing is there when you pass on. . . . The swing, sir . . . is like the blue in the sky, immutable, eternal, indeed transcendental.

GOLF IN WRITING

I READ ABOUT GOLF, with great pleasure, long before I
played it. In one or two of Agatha Christie's mysteries,
which my adolescent self consumed almost as fast as he
consumed slices of raisin bread, murder takes place on the
links; and I conceived of shadowy green stretches where
thin men with thin sticks pursued, at a dignified pace, dark
thoughts and a small white ball. It was P. G. Wodehouse,
however, who brought me resoundingly into the imaginary world of golf—his wonderful, comical golf stories,
scattered through a number of volumes on the shelves of
the local public library and now conveniently collected in
one volume, *The Golf Omnibus.* I had never held a golf
club or been admitted to one, but I had no trouble, for
some reason, in picturing the verdant scene as the Oldest
Member sits on the terrace of the mythical Marvis Bay
Golf and Country Club:

> A pleasant breeze played among the trees on the terrace
> outside the Marvis Bay Golf and Country Club. It ruffled
> the leaves and cooled the forehead of the Oldest Member,

who, as was his custom of a Saturday afternoon, sat in the shade on a rocking chair, observing the younger generation as it hooked and sliced in the valley below. . . . One [golfer] is zigzagging about the fairway like a liner pursued by submarines. Two others seem to be digging for buried treasure, unless—it is too far off to be certain—they are killing snakes. The remaining cripple, who has just foozled a mashie-shot, is blaming the caddie. His voice, as he up-braids the innocent child for breathing during his up-swing, comes clearly up the hill.

"Hook," "slice," "foozle," "mashie"—the words transparently glistened on the page as if I had always known them, just as I had already, in some prior existence, secreted in my childish heart the bliss that Wodehouse expressed in these opening sentences: "It was a morning when all nature shouted 'Fore!' . . . The fairway, as yet unscarred by the irons of a hundred dubs, smiled greenly up at the azure sky; and the sun, peeping above the trees, looked like a giant golf-ball perfectly lofted by the mashie of some unseen god and about to drop dead by the pin of the eighteenth."

I had no difficulty, either, in following the ups and downs of those mock-epic Wodehousian matches, often played for the hand of a comely girl but sometimes for stakes as extravagant as three railroads against an English butler, as in the rousing duel between the American millionaires Bradbury Fisher and Gladstone Bott. Wodehouse superbly evokes golfing style in all its grotesque variety: "Gladstone Bott . . . fussed about for a few moments like a hen scratching gravel, then with a stiff quarter-swing sent his ball straight down the fairway for a matter of seventy yards, and it was Bradbury Fisher's turn to drive." Bradbury Fisher, though like Bott a twenty-four-handicapper, takes quite a different approach: "It was his habit, as a rule, to raise his left foot some six inches from the ground and, having swayed forcefully back on to his right leg, to sway sharply forward again and lash out with sickening violence in the general direction of the ball." Rereading these old frolics with an experienced eye, I see that Wodehouse, like Ring Lardner on baseball, is on solid ground, and never makes a descriptive mistake. There is a great deal of sound advice embedded in the comedy: "Keep your heid still," the Scots pro McHoots tells the tyro Vincent Jopp. "Keep yer ee on the ba'. Dinna press." Wodehouse's grasp of the strange joy and fascination of the game is absolute. His tale of the Fisher-Bott match holds this memorable insight: "Like all twenty-four-handicap men, [Fisher] had the most perfect confidence in his ability to beat all other twenty-four-handicap men." A golfer now for nearly thirty years, with a hard-won and precarious handicap of eighteen, I recognize the rueful truth of that unfounded but irrepressible optimism. Bradbury Fisher is a true golfer also in the faith he reposes in the written word. Before his match with Bott, he "read for a while portions of that grand chapter in James Braid's *Advanced Golf* which deals with driving into the wind. It was a fair and cloudless morning, but it was as well to be prepared for emergencies."

Once launched, in my mid-twenties, upon the actualities of the game so winningly portrayed by Wodehouse, I of course read many books of advice: Armour, Hogan, Palmer, Jones. I pondered pronation, "square-to-square," and the vagaries of the left heel. I faithfully perused a very informative comic strip, *Mac Divot*, that has regrettably, due to some twist of syndication, faded from my ken. I acquainted myself with the fabled lore of the game, with such British giants as Old Tom Morris, Young Tom Morris, Harry Vardon, and Joyce Wethered. I relived, hole by hole, the drama of the epochal Vardon, Ray, and Ouimet playoff, which put American golf forever on the map, and, as the barren months of each winter stretched long, consoled myself vicariously with the pages of such silver-tongued bards of the game as Bernard Darwin and Herbert Warren Wind. I even took note of golf poetry, an unabundant genre that includes Eliot's haunting lines (from his "Choruses from 'The Rock' ")

> And the wind shall say: "Here were decent godless people:
> Their only monument the asphalt road
> And a thousand lost golf balls"

and the exquisite "Seaside Golf," by John Betjeman, of which these are the middle two stanzas:

> And down the fairway, far along
>   It glowed a lonely white;
> I played an iron sure and strong
>   And clipp'd it out of sight,
> And spite of grassy banks between
> I knew I'd find it on the green.
>
> And so I did. It lay content
>   Two paces from the pin;
> A steady putt and then it went
>   Oh, most securely in.
> The very turf rejoiced to see
> That quite unprecedented three.

But none of these literary delights, authentic as all were, explained to me the friendly mystery of why golf itself was such a delight, such a bottomlessly interesting recreation; this philosophical question awaited its elucidation until I was directed to an obscure tome entitled *The Mystery of Golf*, by Arnold Haultain.

The author himself is something of a mystery man. To quote Herbert Warren Wind: "Haultain, one gathers, was a Canadian belle-lettrist, born in 1857, who wrote authoritatively on a wide variety of topics from Cardinal Newman to love." *The Mystery of Golf* was first published in 1908, in a limited edition of four hundred copies, and then republished in a general edition in 1910. To this second edition Haultain added a hundred additional pages of text, thickening the already rich texture of the prose with yet more quaint learning and fancy writing, with more foreign phrases, leisurely ruminations, metaphysical and physiological lore, and references to such worthies as St. Paul, Tennyson, and Yrjö Hirn. The text of the first edition (quaintly adorned with marginalia in Elizabethan English) already more than sufficiently elaborated Haultain's few basic points, in the half-facetious, generously allusive style of turn-of-the-century essayistic writing.

The book's core, however, is pure gold; with an analytical ardor that, as he says, only a tyro of mature years could have mustered (for the young beginner would not be so analytical, and the seasoned player not quite so ardent), Haultain goes to the heart of golf's peculiar lovability and enduring fascination. His shrewdest point comes early:

> . . . there is no other game in which these three fundamental factors—the physiological, the psychological, and the social or moral—are so extraordinarily [the second edition substitutes "intimately"] combined or so constantly called

into play. . . . In no other game that I know of is, first, the whole anatomical frame brought into such strenuous yet delicate action at every stroke; or, second, does the mind play so important a part in governing the actions of the muscles; or, third, do the character and temperament of your opponent so powerfully affect you as they do in golf. To play well, these three factors in the game must be most accurately adjusted, and their accurate adjustment is as difficult as it is fascinating.

In no other sport, that is, does the player so continuously and closely have to perform as his own coach. "Every stroke," Haultain tells us, "must be played by the mind—gravely, quietly, deliberately." In no other sport are mental effort and concentration so immediately reflected in the mirror of physical action and its result. The tennis player crouched on the back line, the baseball pitcher on the mound certainly exhort themselves and inwardly rehearse some technical points; but they can also depend to a large degree upon natural ability and instilled reflex. Golf, it seems, must be learned afresh each time we tee off, and if on the one hand it humbles us with a sudden collapse of some aspect of play we thought had been mastered, it on the other always holds out, perhaps even more to the inept than to the expert, the hope of dramatic improvement. Haultain lucidly extols the fluid, multiform, neo-Platonic complexity of golf as a mental and—though his recurring emphasis on moral fibre as well as mental focus will strike us as old-fashioned—spiritual experience.

Those who can, do; and those who cannot, theorize. Out of his presumed embarrassments in practice Haultain developed a profound grasp of golf's lovely tensions. The chronic debate over whether the stroke is a swing or a hit is resolved in this sentence, worthy of memorization: "It is in fact a subtle combination of a swing and a hit; the 'hit' portion being deftly incorporated into the 'swing' portion just as the head of the club reaches the ball, yet without disturbing the regular rhythm of the motion." He troubles to express, too, the elegant paradox of the starkly simple objective toward which golf's many tools and advisements and wayward incidents all tend: "to knock a ball into a hole—that seems the acme of ease." The late nineteenth century's Darwinian obsessions sharpened Haultain's awareness of the elemental combat beneath golf's genteel formalities—combat in which the human opponent is only the secondary enemy, the primary foe being "great Nature herself" in the guise of the course. He is an eloquent poet of the golf course, and his concluding paragraph is rapturous:

> But may not also the simple delights of the game and its surroundings, with their effect upon the mind and the emotions, be included under the allurements and the mystery of golf? My knowledge of links up to the present is limited, but on mine there are delights which, to me a duffer, are like Pisgah sights: hills, valleys, trees, a gleaming lake in the distance . . . the great breeze that greets you on the hill, the whiffs of air—pungent, penetrating—that come through green things growing, the hot smell of pines at noon, the wet smell of fallen leaves in autumn, the damp and heavy air of the valleys at eve, the lungs full of oxygen, the sense of freedom on a great expanse, the exhilaration, the vastness, the buoyancy, the exaltation . . . And how beautiful the vacated links at dawn, when the dew gleams untrodden beneath the pendant flags and the long shadows lie quiet on the green; when no caddie intrudes upon the

still and silent lawns, and you stroll from hole to hole and drink in the beauties of a land to which you know you will be all too blind when the sun mounts high and you toss for the honour!

Haultain has proven not quite correct in his prophecy that golf "will never be spoiled by professionalism; at least it will never be played by highly-paid professionals for the delectation of a howling and betting mob." The mobs do not howl, but they sigh and cheer, and tournament courses have added bleachers, and gate-money is part of the deal. His sense of golf as an exhilarating combat with an untamable Nature might be dulled, I fear, by a look at today's new courses, with their watered and weedless fairways, flowerbed-lined tees, and embankments built of railroad ties. "There is enormous *chance* in golf," Haultain writes. "There must be, when you propel a cubic inch of gutta-percha over acres of soil." His confidence that golf courses will never become billiard tables and that chance will healthily affect even the proficient player might be shaken by what bulldozers and sprinkler systems have imposed upon patches of the American wilderness. Modern rules, too, conspire against the genial misrule of chance. The average golfer nowadays will not accept a lie in a fairway divot any more than he accepts one on a sprinkler head; and "winter rules" informally obtain even through the lushness of July. Haultain tells of a chivalrous young lady who cleaned the mud off her opponent's ball on the green; this tale loses point when everyone legally picks up and cleans the ball on the green. Quite often we see, on the televised tournaments, the ball marked and dusted for the second putt as well, which is carrying the war against chance to the microscopic level. Money and the masses—

" 'Arry and 'Arriet," as the class-conscious author puts it—have certainly had their leveling effects upon the game of stalwart Man versus rugged Nature that Haultain so loftily depicts.

Golf's innocent heart, however—the lively tugging between the "motor" and "ideational" centers that occurs when we set ourselves, club in hands, over the ball—remains unchanged, along with the soaring flight of a well-struck shot and the welcome rattle of a purposefully executed putt. Haultain introduces the term "kinaesthesis" to denote the portion of the sport that in the end must be relegated to "feel," to intuition of a deep physical kind, and also to suggest the portion of our pleasure that relates to the unparalleled (except in riflery) amounts of space with which a golfer must contend. The variety of strokes, from the forward-bounding drive to the backward-skipping sand wedge, plus all the improvised punches and cuts that our mortal straying forces upon us, composes one of the game's inexhaustible charms. But Haultain says it best:

> In golf you get the whole gamut of the muscular sense, from the gigantic swipe at the tee to the gentle tap on the green. It is called into play at every stroke, and it differs with every difference of club—its weight, its length of shaft, the angle which its face subtends to the horizon, its rigidity or flexibility, the construction and material of its head.—Golf, in short, is a sort of Gargantuan jugglery, a prodigious prestidigitation, a Titanic thimble-rigging, a mighty legerdemain.

For all its sober, relentless numerical aspect, golf affords the player magical sensations, under the skies, amid the magnitudes of space and chance, and this, its curious central ecstasy, has never been more thoughtfully addressed than in these pages composed by an erudite Canadian tyro when our old century was young. Amid the torrents of writing that have entertained golfers, Haultain's essay retains the freshness of a mountain spring.

U.S. GOLF

WHEN I WAS ASKED to speak to you this evening,* my first thought was, "Oh, no—my golf is not nearly good enough!" But then I reflected that one of the charms of the game is that nobody's golf, not even Fred Couples' and Nick Faldo's and Laura Davies', is good enough— good enough to please them and their supporters all the time. Golf is a game that almost never fails, even at the highest levels on which it can be played, to mar a round with a lapse or two, and that at the other extreme rarely fails to grant even the most abject duffer, somewhere in his or her round, with the wayward miracle of a good shot. I am here—I have written over the years so much about the game—because I am curiously, disproportionately, undeservedly happy on a golf course, and perhaps we are all here for much the same reason.

---

*At the One Hundredth Anniversary Celebration of the USGA, held in and around the Temple of Dendur at the Metropolitan Museum of Art, New York City, on December 8, 1994.

We are assembled, specifically, to celebrate the one hundredth anniversary of the United States Golf Association. In the beautiful book observing this centennial, *Golf: The Greatest Game,* John Strawn's chapter on the history of the USGA was fascinatingly informative. The organization was founded, essentially, by a champion golfer, Charlie Macdonald, who resented a ruling and rough conditions which cost him a victory in the first American golf championship, played in Newport in 1894. Once the USGA had been founded, in the words of its first meeting's minutes, "to promote the interests of the game of golf" and "to establish and enforce uniformity of the Rules of the game," Charlie Macdonald was able to win the first official Amateur Championship, again at Newport, in 1895. Like the Church of England, then, the USGA was founded to ease one man's dissatisfactions; and the continuity in its Executive Committee, whose overlapping membership goes back to Macdonald, suggests an episcopal laying on of hands.

Mr. Strawn points out, too, that from quite early on American golf differed in some particulars from its parent golf in Scotland and England. What was there a game of the people, played on otherwise worthless links land, became here a game for gentleman, played at private country clubs. And yet a democratic sense of fairness, we read, dictated the eventual demise of the stymie, and the rise of the dainty custom of cleaning and marking your ball on the green. Primordial golf was a rough-and-ready game, wherein nothing but a club touched the ball between tee and holing out; you took the terrain and your luck as they came. But in the New World, the ideal of human perfectibility favored medal play over match play, and precise and faithful scorekeeping encouraged ever more impeccable golf-course conditions.

I wonder, one hundred years after Charlie Macdonald cried out for some rules and course standards, whether we Americans aren't in danger of taking golf too seriously— too mechanistically. The Canadian writer Arnold Haultain, in his book *The Mystery of Golf,* perhaps the first extended literary meditation upon the game, evokes a humble golf course thus:

> Certain links I know, far away on a western continent, a nine-hole course, miles from train or tram. Club-house there is none; you throw your covert coat and your hat over a fence and—play. There are no greens, there are no flags: the player more familiar with the ground goes ahead and gives you the line. The teeing-grounds are marked by the spots where the soil has been scraped by the boot for the wherewithal for tees. Bunkers abound, and bad lies, in the form of hoof-marks and cart-ruts, do much more abound. . . . Yet . . . to these links, daily gaily trudge ardent golfers, carrying clubs under a sub-arctic August sun.

Haultain, even the rhapsodic rhythm of his prose tells us, was happy on this homely course, and we might ask ourselves if our own happiness would be significantly diminished if our own courses had less than four different well-mown teeing areas, each framed by flowerbeds, and if the yardage figures were not inscribed on the sprinkler heads, and if the greens were a tad less smooth than pool tables, and if players without a medical certificate were forbidden to ride golf carts, and if metal woods were banned? Would American golf fall into irremediable melancholy if manufacturers ceased coming up with new lines of ever more ingeniously weighted and shafted clubs, with which pro shops can churn their clientele into an annual lather of technology-based hope? Would American golf, in short, be less happy if a bit less money were to wash through the grand old game?

We were all pleased, I am sure, to see, the other Sunday, on the televised Skins Game, Tom Watson sink a putt worth $170,000. But was it the number of dollars that cheered us, or the fact that success had finally attended the long-balky putter of one of the few pros who—Trevino and Palmer and Fuzzy Zoeller are others—suggest in their bearing and demeanor that golf is some kind of fun as well as a high-stakes ordeal for poker-faced perfectionists?

When did American golf come of age? Some might say in 1904, when Walter Travis won the British Amateur Championship, the first foreigner to do so. Some might pinpoint the 1920s and the international admiration and affection won by the great Bobby Jones. But perhaps most would specify the happy moment in September of 1913 when the unknown twenty-year-old Francis Ouimet beat the two foremost British players, Harry Vardon and Ted Ray, for the U.S. Open Championship—an upset victory that made news, not just golf news. The moment is commemorated by a USGA Centennial logo, based on a well-known photograph. Look at it; what do we see? Two figures, one of them our heroic golfer, a workingman's son who happened to live in a modest house across from the Country Club in Brookline, Mas-

sachusetts. He picked up golf balls on his way to school, he watched the matches across the street, a member gave his older brother some cast-off clubs, the young Ouimets fell in love with the game. Francis played without fuss. Needing, on the eighteenth green in the last regulation round, to sink a five-foot putt to enter a playoff with the Englishmen, he rapped it at the back of the cup without a second look. The next day, in the playoff, he calmly beat Vardon by five strokes and Ray by six. And who is the other figure in our logo, a little figure? He is Ouimet's caddie, a local ten-year-old called Eddie Lowery, carrying a canvas bag that looks to hold about eight clubs. Think of the caddies in today's championships — burly yardage statisticians toting bags the size of small sofas, loudly blazoned with manufacturers' names for the greedy eyes of the television cameras.

We have come a long way in American golf, but has it been a journey without a price? Amid the million-dollar tournaments and the multi-million-dollar clubhouses, might we be losing the elemental charm of the game itself? An out-of-doors simplicity lies at the heart of golfing bliss, as we are reminded by our logo of two New England boys out for a walk on a drizzly September day. All it takes, in truth, for a golfer to attain his happiness is a fence rail to throw his coat on, and a target somewhere over the rise.

TELEVISION GOLF

WITHOUT EVER ATTENDING a U.S. Open, I have a lot of
vivid Open memories—Arnold Palmer thrashing out of the
bushes on his way to blowing a seven-shot lead over Billy
Casper in the last round of the 1966 Open at Olympic;
Tom Watson chipping in on the par-three at Pebble
Beach in 1982; Hale Irwin staggering home through the
rough at Inverness in 1979; Andy North chunking his last
chip into a trap at Cherry Hills but saving par with a long
uphiller; and Julius Boros right here* twenty-five years
ago, sauntering to victory with a swing so casual it looked
as if he were flicking a swagger stick. These memories
were accumulated, of course, via television, which is the
way most of us watch golf.

No sport is as much improved for the spectator by television as golf. Rather than scurrying from here and there
among the ropes and marshals and straining for a peek

---

*At the Country Club in Brookline, Massachusetts, hosts of the 1988
U.S. Open, for whose program this piece was written.

over the heads of hundreds of other spectators, one sits at ease and sees shot after shot in close-up. Attending a tournament in person, one is rarely in the right place, where the roar goes up as the eagle putt snakes in. On television, that putt is replayed in slow motion, with blade-by-blade analysis of the green by the network turf expert. As the camera coverage becomes ever more sophisticated, all eighteen holes are available to the director, who feeds the screen a constant diet of crisis—of putts missed or made, of drives off-line or down the middle, of irons dead on the flag or drifting, yes, oops, into the bunker. All this, plus helicopter views and video graphics of each hole, charming English voices whispering into the microphone, Lee Trevino giving tips in his friendly Texas twang, twelve-second interviews with this or that personable new blond pro ("I just come out to do my best each week, and I leave the rest of it up to the Lord"), and irresistible commercials for Cadillacs and E. F. Hutton. In answer to the wife's third and most irritated call to Sunday supper, one rises up from the sagging couch bloated with golf, dazed and bedazzled by the beauty of the game, the slickness of the greens, the smoothness of the swings, the gaudiness of the slacks, the lavishness of the purse, and the manicured glory of the eucalyptus trees, or Georgia pines, or royal palms, or whatever they were.

And yet, something is missing from golf as experienced on television. The third dimension is missing. The serene space of it all, and the singing flight of the happily struck shot. On television, every shot appears to jump off to the right, like the worst sort of shank. Again and again one is amazed to be told that the shot that just went sideways off the screen is right on line—that, far from a shank, it has wound up ten feet from the pin. Also, the distances are impossible to judge on the little screen, so that players take 9-irons for what look like targets in the next county. And the greens don't show their slope or swales, so that the putts move in a weird magnetic field insulated from the contours that would be obvious if we were there. Being there, really, is much of the joy of golf—the walks and waits between shots, the textures and smells of the out-of-doors, the haptic reality of the clubs. Golf is only partly visual; an approach putt is stroked, after much looking, by *feel*, and if too much left-brain input interferes with right-brain intuition, the putt is apt to come up short or run long. Television reduces golf to a two-dimensional spectacle as skin-deep, finally, as a pornographic film; in its tendency to show golf as a series of putts that go in the hole or not, television presents a complicated, pleasurable activity stripped of foreplay, feeling, and the vast terrestrial and atmospheric context that corresponds, in this possibly overextended metaphor, to courtship.

There is no substitute, in golf, for playing it. Though mild-mannered men, and even women, have been known to become enthralled by football without ever having felt the thud of a body block or the leathery caress of a good catch, and though boxing and wrestling certainly have their purely voyeuristic audiences, it is hard to imagine an utter non-golfer caringly watching golf for more than a minute or two. We watch television golf, I think, in hopes of improving our own games. Indeed, a feasible mental exercise, on the course, is to imagine oneself to be Weiskopf or Snead or some other champion whose swing we have visually absorbed. By imitating an admired swing at the top of the takeaway and at the end of the follow-through, one stands a fair chance of performing the intermediate steps correctly and hitting the ball with a novel authority.

If this exercise seems too naïvely magical, at least chronic observation of the golfers on television should reinforce a few basic swing thoughts. They *always* bend their knees and sit down to the ball at address, rather than stooping over it stiff-legged. They *always* turn their backs to the hole, freely, without the duffer's fear of losing track of where he is. They do *not*, in that crucial split-second of downswing, anxiously hit with the hands and arms, but instead move the left hip and let the big muscles drag the little ones into the moment of impact. With irons, they always take a decided divot. They always finish, if not high, at least forward, rather than with their weight still on the right foot and the arms wrapped across their chests. In the sand trap, they swing rather than gouge down at the ball in our desperate way, our eyes shut tight against the fearful explosion. On the green, heads solemnly still, they stroke the ball rather than, as we do, stab at it and simultaneously look up in a sheepish agony of hope.

Within the limits of these perennial lessons, television golf offers a reassuring variety of workable styles. The faithful viewer sees that one can play at the highest level even with a hitch in one's backswing as pronounced as Calvin Peete's, or a funny skyward-pointing position at the apogee like George Burns's or Miller Barber's, or an arc as flat as Trevino's, or a temper as impatient as Craig Stadler's, or a loop like Fuzzy Zoeller's or Raymond Floyd's. Not all the swings in golf heaven are pretty, and some that are pretty remain in purgatory, due to mortal failings of faith, zeal, competitive edge, and mental concentration. But, in general, if you can swing like Sam Snead or Curtis Strange* you will do better than by mimicking Arnold Palmer (he punches the ball, and pulls back his follow-through) or Tom Watson (sweet, but so quick). Television golf, like television politics, enables us to sit and judge our betters, and to ask ourselves, "Why them and not me?"

If our attention wanders while watching golf on the tube, and we start sneaking naps or clicking over to the Classic Movies channel, this may answer the question. The men who excel at golf do not let their attentions wander. By the time we see them in the tournament, they have played in Wednesday's pro-am, had a Tuesday warm-up round with their peers or their agents, and perhaps put on a Monday exhibition match somewhere en route. In addition, they have hit out hundreds of practice balls and taken a lesson by long-distance telephone from their old college coach back at Wake Forest. This would be a sickening diet for those of us to whom golf is the dessert of life.

We are also distinguished, we non-professionals, by the secret will to lose. Haven't you ever noticed yourself, when leading by an unconscionable amount in a Wednesday match, beginning to hit bad shots accidentally on purpose? Or panicking three-quarters of the way through a good round and racking up three triple bogeys in a row, because you know you're not that good? Or getting bored with being on the fairway and slicing into the woods just to keep the game interesting? The golfers we see on tele-

---

*Who won, in the event, the 1988 U.S. Open. His name was *not* inserted after the fact.

vision never get bored by their own steady play, never get tired of being on the green in regulation, never rebel against repeating the same workable swing. Even when we switch them off, they keep on playing. And that is why they are inside the little box making millions, and we are on the outside making a deep dent in the davenport.

MEMOIRS OF A MARSHAL

THOUGH A NORMALLY, I suppose, ambitious individual, I never aspired to be a marshal at a U.S. Open. The honor ferreted me out in 1988, when a rustic golf club north of Boston, of which I am a recessive member, was invited to supply marshals to the seventh hole at the Country Club in Brookline. Volunteers were sought. How could one say no? For a mere hundred dollars, I acquired a badge admitting me to every round, a pair of ecru golf slacks, a sexy green-and-white-striped T-shirt, a snappy hat that hurt my head, and a slick green rain windbreaker with a squirrel emblazoned thereupon, like the jacket of a Los Angeles street gang.

My first day on the job came on Wednesday, when the touring pros enjoyed a practice round and autograph-seekers and celebrity-junkies enjoyed limited access to these godlike eminences. The twosome of Jack Nicklaus and Greg Norman was the most awesome, and a frenzied herd accompanied them from hole to hole; when the moment came for the charismatic duo to move from the safety of the seventh green to that of the eighth tee, we marshals formed a protective phalanx around them, and I shall not soon forget the sensation of being a small part of a moving human wall. My feet were trampled and perforated by the cleated shoes of the other marshals, all of whom seemed to be younger and burlier than I, while the two bright-pink faces of the superstars grimaced and bobbed in the middle of our shuffling, grunting mass. Nicklaus, miraculously, even managed to sign a few autographs, as books and programs were thrust at him over our heads and into the cracks of daylight between our ears.

Once the tournament began, the players existed upon another plane, at least in theory. When one pro, whose face was familiar but whose name escaped me, turned to us on the tee and said the water cooler was set too low and somebody would split his pants bending over to it, we were all too stunned to reply or make a move. In exasperation he lifted the two-ton cooler himself and slammed it down on a bench. One more peril of the tour had been revealed to me: split pants.

Holding the ropes one afternoon, I heard Lee Trevino as he went by talking Spanish, as animatedly as he talks English, to Seve Ballesteros's caddie/brother. What a guy! I wondered if he could also speak Japanese to Jumbo Osaki. I was moved; I had heard America singing. But most of the hours passed in a sunstruck stupor, especially when I had the assignment of manning the ropes down in a treeless valley about midway between the tee and the green, a no-man's land pounded, over the days, into a

shimmering dust bowl by the myriad footsteps of spectators. I emerged from the valley feeling microwaved, and
as powdery as a sugar doughnut.

Duty by the green of our long par-three was the most
pleasant. There were shade trees, and chatty spectators
behind the ropes, and occasionally one could importantly
hustle over to guard a stray drive until the player claimed
it, with a nod of terse thanks. I remember how strangely
trivial a golf ball looked in this interim, resting between
strokes, like the weary face of an actor relaxing offstage.
One moment, the spotlight focus of multitudes, and the
next, a lowly orb half-hidden in the anonymous grass.
This sensation of being backstage—hearing the players
sigh, seeing their sweat, feeling the lull on the other side
of the high-energy moments memorialized in headlines
and record books—made being a marshal worthwhile.
When the Open comes around to Brookline again, I'll
sign up for duty on the bench, next to that water cooler.

WOMEN'S WORK

THE ALLEGED HABITATION of the Amazons grew increasingly remote as the ancient Greeks' knowledge of geography widened. At first, they lived and did battle, according to the *Iliad*, in Phrygia and Lycia; in the *Aethiopis* a contingent of them comes from Thrace. When the Black Sea was colonized, the rumored territory of the warrior-women was pushed outward, to Themiscyra on the Thermodon River. Herodotus tells the story of how the Amazons, driven from the Thermodon, sailed to Lake Maeotis, and eventually settled in far Scythia. In the sixteenth century of the Christian era, the Spanish explorer Francisco de Orellana thought he had encountered them on the mighty South American river to which he gave their name. And now we have come to the Salem Country Club* in search of these fabulous creatures.

The Amazons were anciently said to have cut off their

---

*Site of the 1984 USGA Women's Open Championship, for whose official program these reflections were composed.

right breasts, the better to draw the strings of their bows. In today's competitions, they wear gloves only on their left hands, the better to grip their slippery wands of hollow steel. Classic sculptors bodied them forth in the light clinging dress of Artemis, girt high so as not to hamper their running; on late-painted vases they are wearing close-fitting trousers and a high cap called the *kidaris*. Our modern Amazons wear golf skirts that expose their knees, or, increasingly (and increasingly short), shorts; on their curly heads visors protect their delicate faces from the cruel sun in which their sport must be pursued.

It is a cruel sight, in fact, to see these women warriors toiling up and down the hills, their feminine faces creased by too much weather and by the fierce squint of concentration. One expects them to smile more; women are usually smiling, with or without a reason. But our Amazons are doing authentic battle, for heavy stakes and national glory, and their eyes, pale in their tan faces, intent in the shadows of their visors, estimate the distance to the green or the amount of break in the putt with that same pain of calculation which mathematicians and sailors and male golfers feel. There is no rescuing anyone from the vortex of a golf round, and our gallant feelings hang back helpless behind the spectator ropes.

A man at a women's golf tournament, let's face it, is a bundle of mixed emotions. Among these emotions may be distinguished:

(1) Adoration and wonder, that such beauties, many of them slender and, in the writer's case, young enough to be his daughter, could handily trounce him in this game of vaulting distances and iron nerves.

(2) Self-contempt, that this should be so.

(3) That strange, sensuous pleasure a man derives from the sight of women fighting, even when it's not over him. The legend of the Amazons, it seems plausible to conjecture, is a mythologized projection of the male yearning for female aggression, beginning with the hope that his mother will fiercely protect him and maturing into his bitter regret that society has handed him the active role in courtship and mating, a role he is apt to botch. The powerful female is a profoundly pleasing archetype, especially when society has done what it can to make women powerless. The nineteenth century named itself Victorian after a woman, and up from its muffled domestic bondage rose Florence Nightingale, George Eliot, and Madame Blavatsky. As we approach the end of *this* century, the image of the ideal woman has taken on a certain athletic edge; feminist militancy has been deflected into mixed doubles and aerobic dancing. Yet something in us, us men, is scandalized and thrilled by the sight of women competing in deadly earnest.

(4) Attentiveness and humble hope. The average male golfer has much to learn from the female swing: it is so obviously a swing, rather than a stab, push, or clout. A man doing everything wrong, stancewise, can still move the ball a fair distance with just his forearms, wrists, and thumbs; a woman must use her big muscles and swing the club in rhythm, and so should we all. The straightness of the drives in a women's tournament is a particular marvel, much to be envied and emulated. The graceful calm of most of the strokes says louder than words, "Let the club do the work."

(5) A sense of rejection. This bevy of competitors will move on, like a flock of gorgeous but ravenous birds, to

another field next week, to glean the prize money and establish a new pecking order. This is in character. Herodotus reports that the Amazons, offered marriage by an army of be-smitten Scythians, responded, "We dread the prospect of settling down here, for we have done much damage to the country by our raids." They made a counteroffer: "If you wish to keep us for your wives and to behave as honorable men, go and get from your parents the share of property which is due to you, and then let us go off and live by ourselves." For, they explained, "Your women stay at home in their wagons occupied with feminine tasks, and never go out to hunt or for any other purpose."

Whereas, said the Amazons to the pining Scythians, "Our business is with the bow and the spear, and we know nothing of women's work."

IS LIFE TOO SHORT FOR GOLF?

THE SUBJECT OF CROSSWORD PUZZLES had come up at the luncheon table. "Life is too short," I brusquely opined, "for crossword puzzles."

"Yes," the affable young lady at my left eagerly agreed, "for crossword puzzles and for golf." Then her eyes widened in slight social alarm, as she remembered, perhaps, that I had once or twice put myself on record as a faithful if fault-ridden devotee of the game.

"It does take a lot of time," I gracefully conceded, and she mastered her blush, and we moved on to less potentially combustible topics.

But the exchange made me think. How much of my life had I spent playing golf, and could I now estimate, as my life draws near to its final accounting, whether or not this fraction had been ill-spent? Compared with many golfers, of course, I have not spent much time at it at all. For my first twenty-five years, when many a country-club lad and lassie were honing their skills and toasting their noses on a sun-drenched links from March to November, I invested not a minute in the pastime, instead spending long hours failing to guess the murderer in mystery novels, learning how to draw with a split-nib pen without smudging, and mastering the nuances, in the company of other adolescent idlers, of such unprofitable sports as box hockey, roof ball, pinball, and single-basket basketball. In the fullness of manhood I took up golf, figuring that, now that I was a free-lance writer, I should do something with my afternoons.

My afternoons, back then, seemed freer than now, though the time I spend trying to cover blank paper is much the same. But in those days there was less mail to answer, the phone rang less often, there were no speaking engagements to fulfill, fewer proofs to ponder, fewer favor-seekers to placate—much less marginalia, that is, to the text of my vocation. I had small children and worked at home and needed now and then to get out of the house. Golf was a sport one could play alone and practice alone. And then, after dark, one could read about it, searching for that magic tip, that single all-unlocking swing thought which would transmute the dross of ineptitude into one golden sweet shot after another.

The game had its instant fascinations for me. The difference between a good shot and a bad shot was marvellously large, and yet the difference between a good swing and a bad seemed microscopically small. Even from the start, I could now and then hit a shot that felt and looked thrillingly right. Yet, as the hours and the summers on the golf course mounted in number, I seemed as far as ever from discovering how to hit such shots all the time. Or even half the time. The fluctuations of golfing success

were charted on a graph craggier than those of other en-
deavors, with peaks of pure poetry leaping up from
abysses of sheer humiliation—the fat shot that sputters
forward under the shadow of its divot, the thin shot that
skims across the green like a maimed bird, the smothered
hook which finds the raspberry patch, the soaring slice
that crosses the highway, the chunked chip, the shanked
approach, the water ball, the swamp ball, the deeper-into-
the-woods ricochet, the trap-to-trap blast, the total whiff
on the first tee, the double-hit putt from two feet out.
Here was rich sport indeed.

Though the son of a high-school athletic coach, I had
not been much of a boyhood athlete. The natural athletes
of the public schools and playgrounds of my native Pennsylvania left me grovelling in the dirt, in the grass, on the
waxed gymnasium floor. Compared with them I had—
strangely, since I could outsmart them in the classroom—
a tendency to lose my head in the pattern of the basketball
break, or in the shuffle of the backfield, or in the quick-
reflex emergencies of a baseball game. In the lazy striding
of golf, where the ball isn't going anywhere without you,
I felt I had a game I couldn't panic in, and one wherein I
might ruminate my way to prowess. And, though those
old naturals even now could probably beat me swinging
left-handed and three beers to the wind, in the rocky
Transcendentalist pastures of New England I have found
some other spindly types among whom I have won my
share of nassaus and enjoyed a wealth of cheerful competitive thrills. My once-or-twice-a-week golf games have
been islands of bliss in my life, and my golfing companions, whose growing numbers now include a number of

the dead, are more dear to me than I can unembarrassedly say. Somehow, it is hard to dislike a man once you have played a round of golf with him.

The nature of humankind must be considered before we decide what life is too short for. Is it too short for sex, for instance, or is sex its business? Men and women need to play, and it is a misused life that has no play scheduled into it. Crossword puzzles, even, have a fit place in some psychological budgets. With them, as with golf, we set ourselves to solve a puzzle nature has not posed. Nothing in natural selection demands that we learn how to beat a small ball into a hole with a minimum number of strokes.

But, it might be argued, the arrowing nature of the attempt answers to ancient hunting instincts, and the great green spaces of a golf course remember the landscape in which the human animal found his soul. Certainly the sight of our favorite fairway wandering toward the horizon is a balm to the eyes and a boon to the spirit. Our mazy progress through the eighteen is a trek such as prehistoric man could understand, and the fact that the trek is fatiguingly long constitutes part of its primitive rightness. A more reasonable length—twelve holes, say—wouldn't have the resonance, the religious sense of ordeal. It is of the essence that a game of golf can't be quickly over and done with; it must be a journey.

To be sure, there have been days when I regretted having to jump up from my desk, where something valuable seemed to be happening, in order to keep a golf date. There have been moments, while trudging up the slope of the thirteenth hole of an indifferent round on a baked-out summer day, when I wondered what I was doing here. But in fact such moments are few, for it is a rare round without its sudden rewards, its little turns of drama. Four golfers of variable talent, over the course of eighteen holes, will each manage to win the momentary applause of the others. While the game's grand spaces pour ease upon the brain and the optic nerves, the quirky contacts of metal and balata entertain the narrative sense.

As soon say life is too short for sleep as say it is too short for golf. As with dreaming, we enter another realm, and emerge refreshed. Golf turns life inside-out; it rests the overused parts of ourselves, and tests some neglected aspects—the distance-gauging eye, the obscure rhythmic connection between feet and hands. For the hours and days it has taken from me, golf has given me back another self, my golfing self, who faithfully awaits for me on the first tee when I have put aside the personalities of bread-winner and lover, father and son. Golf lengthens life, I should have told that young lady.

THE YANKEE GOLFER

New England, that little six-state conglomerate shaped like a shaggily mittened hand waving good-bye to Europe, would not seem to be very promising territory for the spacious sport of golf. The soil is rocky and the season is brief. In my part of Massachusetts, the determined golfer can venture out onto the muddy, scarcely greening courses in the bitter breezes of April and play until snow falls, generally late in the autumn. On Cape Cod, some courses stay open all winter; in the three northern New England states, the golf season is not much more than an interruption of the ski season.

And yet, unlike the Southwest, we have rain, and, unlike Florida, we have hills. Furthermore, it's a rare summer noon when it's too hot to walk the course. The warm weather comes on in tantalizing stops and starts up to Memorial Day; then it's suddenly lush, with the fairways narrowed by the trees' full leafing. Deciduous trees—oak and maples and hickories—dominate, forming dense walls of green. The rough, not much less hospitable than fairway all spring, thickens with daisies and buttercups and wild-strawberry vines and running raspberries and buffalo grass and the footprints of frustrated ball-hunters. By late June, L.L. Bean corduroys have become Bermuda shorts; layers of sweaters are peeled down to a polo shirt. Little whiffs of dust begin to fly from the divots, and the fairways take on the shine of cart tracks. The lines at the public courses lengthen, and the private clubs mount their tournaments and post their winners, on those charts like a sideways pyramid of tuning forks. New England golf is in summer overdrive.

Midges swarm in May, and mosquitoes and greenhead flies flourish near salt marshes, but the golfer is in no danger from alligators, and the odds are slight that the ball will vanish down a Gila-monster burrow. In a crabbed land of early settlement and urban development, the courses tend to be short—even the Country Club in Brookline, the site of two U.S. Opens since World War II, has to be lengthened by combining several holes of the twenty-seven on the layout. My home course of Myopia, in Hamilton, Massachusetts, hosted four Opens between 1898 and 1908, but, at 6,440 yards, considered itself in need of some deeper back tees. Still, it's plenty long enough for me, and for most of its habitués.

New England rough is grabby. The woods are dense and embellished with poison ivy and greenbrier; playing golf once in Augusta, I marvelled at the comfortable carpet of needles spread beneath the Georgia pines, which presented no more obstacle than well-spaced telephone poles would have. In New England, we poke our way through a landscape man-modified but not man-made— indeed, in some sections little changed since the days of the Puritans, and little mollified for sporting use. The New World did not have links land as easily convertible to golf as the seaside dunes of the British Isles, but a rough-and-ready links ideal hovers over the design of the region's venerable courses, even to the fabrication of grassy mounds like the famous "chocolate drops" to the left of the seventh green at the Country Club. This course, in Brookline, where Ouimet beat Vardon and Ray and, more recently, Julius Boros and Curtis Strange won tightly contested Opens, is the grandest of the old layouts. Its primordial outcroppings of the dark conglomerate formations called puddingstone loom most spectacularly on the eleventh hole, whose name, "The Himalyas," answers to the something timeless, brooding, and benign about this venerated course.

When the Yankee golfer lifts his head from the game, he is greeted by varied vistas—none more beautiful than the immense spread of marsh and beach and tidal river seen from the fourth tee at the Cape Ann course, a public nine-holer. At the Winchester Country Club, one begins by driving steeply uphill, and at Wellesley one finishes both nines on elevated greens with the flags usually out of sight. At the Essex County [sic] Club in Manchester-by-the-Sea, one finishes on the eighteenth by hitting into the sun over a grassy hill and then over a curving blue creek and a bit of marsh for good measure. It's been many years since I played the Sugarbush course in Vermont, but I still recall the sensation of hitting around the mountain, with brushy hillside on the left and the tops of pines on the right of the corkscrewing fairways. The second side of the Colonial course in Lynnfield seems to float an inch above water, like Venice. Bass Rocks, at Rockport, is no misnomer; granite outcroppings jut all over the lot, providing many a startling bounce. Golf in New England rarely fails to deliver, at the least, an entertaining walk in the country.

Autumn brings to the courses an especial beauty. The maples flare a pinkish red, the hickories turn a buttery yellow, the oaks withdraw into a rusty brown. The trees gradually show bare branches and a fresh new breadth of light washes over the fairways. Views deepen; forgotten perspectives reappear. The lower angle of sunlight brings the swellings and swales into fuller relief. The course has been ripening toward this season of golden harvest. The migrating geese honk overhead, the squirrels hustle back and forth with their urgent acorns, and the golfer as he strides briskly along feels alone in a tawny Eden. The young are back in school and the old have retreated to Florida; to the survivors belongs the course, until the first snow falls.

There are some disadvantages to autumnal golf. Drifts of leaves hide errant shots—but, then, a provisional "leaf rule" can be rather generously invoked, to speed play on its way. Curled-up goosefeathers and bits of milkweed do cunning imitations of missing golf balls. In the low light, even the grass can glint like Surlyn. The fairway turf, once frost begins to toy with it, develops a skin of mud. Worm castings become suddenly prominent, and greens aerated in October retain a quilted texture that sends putts a-bobbing. The sand in the traps takes on the consistency of drying cement, and inexorably, as the days pinch in, the grounds crew removes the tee markers, the yardage stakes, and finally the flags. Still, one can hit for the greens and throw down a spare ball to substitute for the

hole: a hole is a bit less than three balls across, so any contact can be considered a sunk putt. On occasion I have
seen one of the group's wallets used for a substitute target.
The wallet can be quite thin; we thrifty Yankees find a dollar nassau, or a quarter-a-point game of Bingo-Bango, about
as much financial excitement as our nerves can tolerate.

In fall a primeval relaxation overtakes the ancient game.
The course conditions, shaggy and casual, revert to those
of the late-medieval motherlands of the sport, called *goff*
by the Scots and *colf* by the Dutch. (The Dutch played the
game with brass-headed *colfsloffen*, or "golf slippers.") Preferred lies are nudged up even in the rough. With the
computers that calculate our handicaps to a decimal fraction shut down for the season, we stop counting, beyond
the modest mathematical needs of a friendly match. Autumn golf is a kind of afterlife, with the summer's severe
reckonings left far behind and our good deeds and bad
blended into a nostalgic haze. A mellow mood of self-
forgiveness prevails above the withering turf. The all-
seeing sun has yielded pride of place to the myopic, milky
moon. The defoliated rough yields up a wealth of balls,
and so many nocturnal creatures scurry through the sand
traps on the way to hibernation that there scarcely seems
a need to rake, even if the rakes weren't already stored in
the equipment shed. With so few other players out on the
course, one moves at one's own pace at last, neither pushing nor being pushed, and crossing from the fourteenth
green to the seventeenth tee in order to finish before
darkness falls.

For the senior golfer, is there not a consoling resonance
in these autumnal rounds? Golf holds out hope of im-

provement longer than any other sport, but does there not come a time when even the most avid collector of tips and lessons must face the fact that his handicap will never be any lower than it is? When a perfectly nailed drive, whizzing forward like a rocket, somehow winds up thirty yards short of the drives of yesteryear? When even the head of the putter seems heavy? When not a thousand dollars' worth of new metal woods engineered by half the geniuses in Texas will stem the inexorable erosion of developed skills? Then the game asks our love not as the repository of infinite possibilities that it once was but as a measure of our finitude. Everything has dwindled but, perhaps, our bliss. The trees are skeletal and silvery, and ghosts of departed partners flutter at our sides, yet the game goes on, this trusty old game of unfailing suspense and surprise. Like an apple stored in a chilly barn, golf is all the sweeter on the edge of winter; each round seems the more precious, in that it may be the last. The last 5-iron to the well-trapped eighteenth, the last lag putt, the last two-footer rattling on the bottom of the cup.

In New England, winter closes down like a casket, abruptly. Cross-country skiers appear on the blanketed fairways, and little boys with sleds gleefully slide downhill where we have labored to drag our bags upward. It seems peculiar, passing on the road, to see the faithless course frozen and glazed, forgetful of all the good times we had together. Fear not: underneath, it keeps its contours and dreams of our returning in the rawness of spring, wearing our windbreakers and long johns and waterproof cleats. New England golf takes character, but character is what it builds.

DECEMBER GOLF

An hour north of Boston, the golf shops hold their end-of-season sales in early October, and by the end of the month the club pros have flown south to Florida, to begin all over again. The courses remain open, however, for a month or so—at first with flags in fresh-cut cups, and then without flags but with unlined holes cut in the middle of the green, and finally with no holes in the green but perhaps temporary greens set up some yards in front, on patches of fairway where putting is as chancy as bowling across cobblestones. Nevertheless, a devoted few play on, through Indian summer and Thanksgiving, into December, until the first snowfall puts a decisive end to the golfing season.

Just as a day may come at sunset into its most glorious hour, or a life toward the gray-bearded end enter a halcyon happiness, December golf, as long as it lasts, can seem the fairest golf of the year. The unkind winds and muddy plugged lies of April and May, the deepening rough of June, the thronging summer folk of July and August, the obfuscating goosefeathers and fallen leaves of the autumn are all gone, gone, and golf feels, on the frost-stiffened fairways, reduced to its austere and innocent essence.

December always holds some mild-enough days. Sunshine glints like a thin shell of ice on the upper side of the bare gray twigs, the sky is striped like blue bacon, a tardy line of Canadian geese wobbles its way south, and the air is delighted to be providing oxygen to some plucky sportsmen. The foursome, thinned perhaps to a mere threesome or twosome, meets by the boarded-up clubhouse, exhilarated to have an entire golf course to itself. Fairway upon fairway are visible through the naked trees, zigzagging back and forth in the view from the first tee. There are no tee markers, no starting times, no scorecards, no electric carts—just golf-mad men, wearing wool hats and two sweaters each, moving on their feet. The season's handicap computer has been disconnected, so the sole spur to good play is rudimentary human competition—a simple best-ball nassau or fifty-cent game of skins, its running tally carried in the head of the accountant or retired banker in the group. You seem to be, in December golf, re-inventing the game, in some rough realm predating its modern refinements.

The ball, even smartly struck, has a deadish sound, and stops twenty yards short of where a summer swing would have placed it. The balls themselves are apt to be those at the bottom of the golf-bag pocket, the scarred and dirty orphans of the season. The clubs, too, with the slaves of the caddie shack all gone back to high school or college, still bear September's grassy residue unscoured from their grooves, and impart but a smudge of backspin. Excuses abound, in short, for not playing very well, and the well-struck shot has a heightened lustre as it climbs through the heavy air and loses itself in the dazzle of the low hibernal sun. Winter rules, of course, legitimize generous relocations on the fairway, and with the grass all dead and matted who can say where the fairway ends? It possibly extends, in some circumstances, even into the traps, where the puddling weather, lack of sand rakes, and foraging raccoons have created conditions any reasonable golfer may take it upon himself to adjust with his foot.

A lovely leniency, that is, prevails in December golf, as a reward for our being out there at all. The course itself—its ice-edged water hazards, its newly erected snow fences—seems grateful to be visited, to have golfers tickling with their cleats and divots the shapely slopes and expanses that in another month will be useful only to cross-country skiers and snowmobiles, scrawling their tracks idiotically across the logic of the layout. There is a misty woodsmoke feeling to the round, the savor of last things.

We are not quite alone. A distant dog-walker ambulates along the seventh fairway. Two urchins armed with sawed-off irons have sneaked into the course at the par-three eleventh, where the fence needs repairing. Three members of the greens crew are out with the pick-up truck on the fifteenth, clearing away that clump of sumac and oak which has swallowed many a foozled drive. In December, thickets that in July seem impenetrable jungle, virulent with poison ivy and greenbrier, become a few sticks and stalks, cleared easily, in an atmosphere of crisp transparency. The rasp of chain saws carries across the course, a distinct distraction on the sixteenth tee, fading to a dim and friendly buzzing when the seventeenth green is reached.

Something about December golf—the bulky clothes, perhaps, or the bare lies, or a fear that the chilly ball might shatter—cramps my swing, I have noticed. The shortening days impose a shorter backswing. I find myself trying to steer the ball, and the shots grow increasingly stunted, and pulled, and displeasing to myself and my partner. It is with a great effort of imagination—a long reach back into the airy warmth of summer—that I remind myself that golf is a game of letting go, of a motion that is big and free. *Throw your hands at the hole,* I tell myself, or, *Turn, you dummy;* and perhaps the shots do begin to click again, and climb in the air that fraction of a second extra, before settling to descend.

But by then the nassau has been decided, and dusk has crept out of the woods into the fairways. The happy flow of banter has cooled. Ice has found its way into your golf shoes; the fingers of your right hand have no feel; your face hurts. Time to pack it in. The radio calls for snow tomorrow. *Throw your hands at the hole.* The last swing feels effortless, and the ball vanishes dead ahead, gray lost in gray, right where the eighteenth flag would be. The secret of golf has been found at last, after seven months of futilely chasing it. Now, the trick is to hold it in mind, all the indoors months ahead, without its melting away.

A Note About the Author

John Updike was born in 1932, in Shillington, Pennsylvania. He graduated from Harvard College in 1954, and spent a year in England, at the Ruskin School of Drawing and Fine Art in Oxford. From 1955 to 1957 he was a member of the staff of *The New Yorker*, to which he has contributed poems, short stories, essays, and book reviews. Since 1957 he has lived in Massachusetts, where he took up golf. His novels have won the Pulitzer Prize, the National Book Award, the American Book Award, the National Book Critics Circle Award, and the Howells Medal.

A Note on the Type

The text of this book was set in a digitized version of Janson, a typeface long thought to have been made by the Dutchman Anton Janson, who was a practicing type founder in Leipzig during the years 1668–1687. However, it has been conclusively demonstrated that these types are actually the work of Nicholas Kis (1650–1702), a Hungarian, who most probably learned his trade from the master Dutch type founder Dirk Voskens. The type is an excellent example of the influential and sturdy Dutch types that prevailed in England up to the time William Caslon developed his own incomparable designs from them.

Composed by N.K. Graphics, Keene, New Hampshire
Printed and bound by The Haddon Craftsmen,
Scranton, Pennsylvania